RUE

URAGE

D1473123

TRUE COURAGE

Emboldened by God in a Disheartening World

STEVE FARRAR

David C Cook®
transforming lives together

TRUE COURAGE
Published by David C Cook
4050 Lee Vance View
Colorado Springs, CO 80918 U.S.A.

David C Cook Distribution Canada
55 Woodslee Avenue, Paris, Ontario, Canada N3L 3E5

David C Cook U.K., Kingsway Communications
Eastbourne, East Sussex BN23 6NT, England

David C Cook and the graphic circle C logo
are registered trademarks of Cook Communications Ministries.

The website addresses recommended throughout this book are offered as a
resource to you. These websites are not intended in any way to be or imply an
endorsement on the part of David C Cook, nor do we vouch for their content.

LCCN 2011920249
ISBN 978-1-4347-6873-5
eISBN 978-1-4347-0365-1

Published in association with the literary agency of WordServe Literary
Group, Ltd., 10152 S. Knoll Circle, Highlands Ranch, CO 80130.

The Team: Don Pape, Larry Libby, Sarah Schultz, Jack Campbell, Karen Athen
Cover Design: Amy Kiechlin
Cover Photo: Getty Images

Printed in the United States of America
First Edition 2011

1 2 3 4 5 6 7 8 9 10

012711

To Lew Spencer,
Race Car Legend
Trusted Friend
Servant of the King

CONTENTS

ACKNOWLEDGMENTS   9

TROUBLED HEARTS AND TRUE COURAGE   11

1. COURAGE TO STAY THE COURSE   25

2. ACTS AND FACTS   53

3. FLUMMOXED AND FLABBERGASTED   79

4. GOLD STANDARD   103

5. LOCK, STOCK, AND BARREL   125

6. THE HARD WAY   151

7. A SLIGHT THING   179

8. IN THE COMPANY OF LIONS   205

NOTES   227

ACKNOWLEDGMENTS

You would not be holding this book in your hands without the work of a dedicated and gifted crew. Special thanks to Dan Rich, Don Pape, Larry Libby, and Jack Campbell. These guys work hard and make books happen that point people to the Lord Jesus Christ. I am privileged to be in the foxhole with them.

Introduction

TROUBLED HEARTS AND

TRUE COURAGE

We are living in disturbing and draining days—days that distress our minds and hearts. Daniel would have understood our distress, because he faced exactly the same thing.

Our nation, as with Daniel's nation so many centuries ago, seems to be collapsing from within. What is required in these days is True Courage. Daniel 11:32 states that "the people who know their God will display strength and take action" (NASB).

That is True Courage.

In every crisis that Daniel faced, he displayed strength and took action—and it was all due to the fact that he *knew* God. There is a wrong kind of action that is ultimately fruitless—but there is a right kind of action that steadies and quiets the heart and gives great hope for the future. Daniel and his friends model this right kind of action in the first six chapters of the book of Daniel. That's why this book is focused entirely on those six chapters. In the pages that follow, we will learn what True Courage really looks like and how it behaves under pressure.

In a nutshell, Daniel displayed True Courage by:

- Fearing God more than man
- Trusting God with his future
- Realizing God's governance over all events

True Courage is the result of knowing God. Only then can a man display strength and take action. And he can do so with a heart that is calm, steady, and at rest—even in the worst of times. That kind of man knows that even when days look their darkest, God has a good plan.

Daniel was one of the Jews in Babylon who had suffered incredible loss. To Daniel and his friends a message came through loud and clear: *"'There is hope for your future,' declares the LORD"* (NASB).

That laser beam of hope found in Jeremiah 31:17 for Daniel and his friends travels at the speed of light to God's people today. "There is hope for your future." That was true not only in Daniel's day; it is also true for us today.

And because it is true, it's the basis for *your* courage.

Discouragement is almost at epidemic levels in these days of economic hardship and political turmoil. Everywhere I look these days I see troubled hearts and troubled minds, sick with worry.

And to those of us who find ourselves with troubled hearts, the Lord Jesus says, "Let not your heart be troubled; you believe in God, believe also in Me" (John 14:1 NKJV).

Those are holy words, sacred words, and not to be used flippantly or taken out of context. The first sentence is not to be separated from the second. If you take the first sentence by itself, you have removed the firing pin.

We are told constantly that we should not be troubled, depressed, or give in to worry. But why shouldn't we give in to worry? Why shouldn't our hearts be troubled? There has to be a *reason* for our hearts not to be troubled. I have heard a well-meaning radio and television personality often say, "Let not your heart be troubled." Yet every time I hear him utter those words, it troubles me. Why? Because he is carelessly quoting only half of the sentence that has the power to calm the seas and troubled hearts. The Lord Jesus had a *reason* why He told His disciples and us, "Let not your heart be troubled." He went on to say, *"You believe in God; believe also in Me."*

That's the answer right there. That's the best reason I can think of why our hearts should never be controlled by fear. The truth is, when the events and circumstances swirling around us seem out of control, they are actually under control.

God the Father, God the Son, and God the Spirit are in complete control of the events taking place in your life, in the life of your nation, and in the life of the entire world. In fact, apart from Him, there would be no life in the universe at this moment.

This is what Paul declared to the Greeks in Acts 17:24–25:

> The God who made the world and everything in it,
> being Lord of heaven and earth, does not live in tem-
> ples made by man, nor is he served by human hands,
> as though he needed anything, since he himself gives
> to all mankind life and breath and everything.

Paul then goes even further in verse 28 and states that "in him we live and move and have our being."

There is the *reason* for an untroubled heart. This is the medicine for whatever might be troubling your heart right now. No matter how hopeless our immediate circumstances, no matter how depressing our future may look, we are to believe in God the Father and His Son. It is the work of the Holy Spirit to turn our troubled hearts to focus on and think about the greatness of the Lord Jesus (John 16:14).

True Courage is found in a heart that believes and trusts in the living God—period.

Yes, we are certainly living in difficult and frightening times. Our nation continues to mock and abandon the principles of God's Word. This is also the case in numerous other nations around the world. Our national downward slide toward immorality continues; and as a result, those who look at life through the lens of Scripture are asking three questions:

- Will we lose our nation?
- Will we lose our liberty?
- Will we lose our free enterprise?

These are biblical questions—and the same questions undoubt-edly asked in Judah when Daniel was just a little boy. The times were different and the terminology was different, but in essence those three questions were on the hearts of the remnant left in the land. When these three questions are being asked, it is a sign that the hearts of the godly are troubled. It was true twenty-five hundred years ago before Daniel and his nation were taken into captivity, and it is true today.

I'm not taking a political position here. I am simply acknowledg-ing why we are seeing so many troubled hearts. None of this is new. We are facing it in our day, and Daniel's parents faced it in their day. This is real life, and it crosses boundaries not only of individual nations but also of centuries.

Allow me to clarify briefly what I mean by "free enterprise," and why it's so important. It may seem out of place in a book about Daniel—but it truly fits into the context. It's important to note that at its very core free enterprise springs from biblical principles. Free enterprise came from something, and what it came from was the Bible. "Free enterprise is the system of values and laws that respects private property, encourages industry, celebrates liberty, limits gov-ernment, and creates individual opportunity. Under free enterprise, people can pursue their own ends—and they reap the rewards and consequences, positive and negative, of their own actions."[1]

Bible scholars J. I. Packer, Merrill Tenney, and William White Jr. make the point:

> [The law given by Moses] encouraged agricultural development among the Hebrew landowners

(Deut. 26:1–11). Farming became an honorable
career as people earned a living by the sweat of their
brows. When the Hebrews entered the Promised
Land, each family received its own allotment of
land. The Law did not permit a family to relinquish
permanent rights to it; it was to remain the family inheritance (Deut. 19:14). The Hebrew farmer
looked upon his land as a gift from God, and he
believed that he was to be a faithful steward of it
(Deut. 11:8–17).[2]

In other words, God granted man with the right to work the
land. His property was not to be taken from him by a king or by
other tribes (Deut. 27:17). God gave him certain rights, and that
included owning and working his property. He was to be a faithful steward in his work. He was not to be a sluggard. He was to
go to Jerusalem three times a year for the feasts to thank God for
His faithful provision of the harvests. But the man had to work and
work hard. God gave him certain rights and liberties to do his work
without tyrannical interference from the governing powers.

Dr. Wayne Grudem is one of the church's most gifted biblical
scholars, and he demonstrates the biblical basis of free enterprise:

> According to the teachings of the Bible, government
> should both document and protect the ownership
> of private property in a nation.

The Bible regularly assumes and reinforces a system in which *property belongs to individuals,* not to the government or to society as a whole.

We see this implied in the Ten Commandments, for example, because the eighth commandment, "You shall not steal" (Exod. 20:15), assumes that human beings will own property that belongs to them individually and not to other people. I should not steal my neighbor's ox or donkey because *it belongs to my neighbor,* not to me and not to anyone else.

The tenth commandment makes this more explicit when it prohibits not just stealing but also *desiring* to steal what belongs to my neighbor:

"You shall not covet your neighbor's house; you shall not covet your neighbor's wife, or his male servant, or his female servant, or his ox, or his donkey, or anything that is your neighbor's" (Exod. 20:17).

The reason I should not "covet" my neighbor's house or anything else is that *these things belong to my neighbor,* not to me and not to the community or the nation.

This assumption of private ownership of property, found in this fundamental moral code of the Bible, puts the Bible in direct opposition to the communist system advocated by Karl Marx. Marx said:

"The theory of the Communists may be summed up in the single sentence: abolition of private property" [Karl Marx, *Communist Manifesto* (New York: International Publishers, 1948), 23].

One reason why communism is so incredibly dehumanizing is that when private property is abolished, government controls all economic activity. And when government controls all economic activity, it controls what you can buy, where you will live, and what job you will have (and therefore what job you are allowed to train for, and where you go to school), and how much you will earn. It essentially controls all of life, and human liberty is destroyed. Communism enslaves people and destroys human freedom of choice. The entire nation becomes one huge prison.[3]

The nation of Judah was about to become a huge prison because of hundreds of years of disobedience to God. Or to be more exact, the nation of Judah was about to go into a Babylonian prison for seventy years. A king/tyrant from Babylon by the name of Nebuchadnezzar was being sent by God to take all of their freedoms and liberties away from them—including their land. And it was in this time that Daniel was born. To put it frankly, his future, from a strictly human standpoint, didn't look too promising. But it is a massive mistake to only look at life from a human perspective and forget the working of the Invisible Hand.

Earlier I mentioned Daniel's parents. This is a book about Daniel, but I have often wondered about his father and mother. The Scriptures tell us nothing about them. But my suspicion (and it's nothing more than that) is that they were godly people. I surmise that for one reason and one reason only: Young teenage boys who display the godly discernment and character that Daniel had at such an early age tend to come from good soil. Daniel's wisdom as a teenager makes me suspect that he had godly parents.

If they were godly people, then they had to be concerned about what the future would bring for their children and grandchildren. If they were godly people, they appreciated that their son Daniel was born under the rule of King Josiah, the greatest king of all the kings of the Old Testament (2 Kings 23:25). Through the leadership of King Josiah, the nation of Judah enjoyed a spiritual revival. But although Josiah fully followed the Lord with a whole heart, most of the people did not.

It was during the time of Josiah that the prophet Jeremiah came on the scene. He told the nation that hard days were coming because of their unbelief and disobedience to the one true God. The nation would be taken into captivity into Babylon for seventy years. If Daniel's parents were godly people, then they were familiar with Jeremiah's preaching (Jer. 1:2–3); therefore, they had to have been concerned about what the future would hold for young Daniel.

Upon the death of Josiah, things began to immediately change for the worse in Judah. Economic prosperity almost immediately disappeared as the throne was handed off to Josiah's son. "Political, social, financial, moral, and spiritual decay led to the country's demise within two short decades."[4] Before long, Nebuchadnezzar, the feared tyrant of Babylon, was in charge. And this was when young Daniel was carried off to Babylon, never to return to Jerusalem again. When that occurred, Daniel lost his nation and his liberty. And when he suffered this great loss, he was right in the middle of God's will.

God abandoned the nation, but God never abandoned Daniel. God never abandons His people, even in times of great distress and tyranny.

A close look at Daniel and God's sovereign care over all of the threats to his life and well-being will serve as a timely transfusion to fight off fear and worry about the days that are ahead. What is needed in our times is not courage—what is needed is *True* Courage.

God put it in Daniel's heart.

He will put it in ours.

One of the traits of True Courage is that it enables you to relax. Psalm 46:10 states it clearly:

> Be still, and know that I am God.
> I will be exalted among the nations,
> I will be exalted in the earth!

When you know that He is God and you ponder what our great God is up to, well, that's when you can begin to relax.

If we were to continue into the second half of Daniel (chapters 7—12), we would find out how God will be exalted among the nations and in the earth. We're not going to study those chapters in this volume—that would be another book entirely. So let me summarize for you what Daniel says is going to happen in the future.

Eventually democracy and free enterprise will be wiped out. The Antichrist will set up and rule through a one-world government. This will all come about in due time, and it cannot be stopped or thwarted, because it is the plan of almighty God. This is where history is going. God has written and ordained it. Read Daniel and Revelation, and you will see that the Lord Jesus will return and defeat and destroy this worldwide government of Satan. Jesus will rule and reign over the new earth from His throne in the New Jerusalem—and His kingdom will endure forever.

This is all coming, and it cannot be delayed or reversed. God is moving the whole world ahead according to His prophetic plan. We are not a minute behind or a minute ahead—we are exactly on pace with God's plan for the ages. His plan is on course and on schedule. That includes the events of yesterday, the events of today, and the events that will happen tomorrow. It's all under His sovereignty.

Things will not get better and better.

They will get worse and worse.

And then the Lord Jesus will return and set it all straight forever.

It is the plan of almighty God, and it is designed that way to bring ultimate good to His people and glory to His name.

In the midst of it all, remember that He has not forgotten about you or your family. So give the Lord Jesus first place in your heart and in your life. His eye is upon you, and He will sustain you. He will make a way when there is no way. Don't be sick with worry. Look to Him! Look to His promises—and know that He is working out His great plan for the ages—and that He will supply every dollar you will need until your dying breath.

Things aren't out of control—they are under control.

That's the concrete of True Courage.

"He has honor if he holds himself to an ideal of conduct though it is inconvenient, unprofitable, or dangerous to do so."

Walter Lippmann

Chapter One

COURAGE TO STAY THE COURSE

True Courage can throw you at first, because it's counterintuitive.

In other words, it's the opposite of what you might *expect*.

My best example? Getting into a pickup and backing up a trailer into the garage. No sweat, you say? What's the big deal about backing a trailer into a garage? It's no sweat until you try to pull it off. If you've never done it before, thirty seconds into it you're sweating like a fire hydrant because that pickup and trailer are twisted like a pretzel—and you're suddenly parked in the flowerbed with no clue how to get out.

Why it is so hard to back up a trailer? It's *counterintuitive,* that's why. If you want the trailer to go left, you don't turn the wheel left. No, if you want to go left, you have to turn to the *right*. If you're going forward and you want to turn left then you turn left—but not if you're backing up. When you're backing up, the rules change, and to get that trailer in the garage you have to go against the grain of what makes sense.

Okay, now let's plow right into Daniel, who right out of the blocks, demonstrates that True Courage is … counterintuitive.

In Daniel 1, we find *two events* that reveal True Courage.

Also in Daniel 1, we discover *three traits* that are the basis of True Courage.

TWO EVENTS
The Crash

"In the third year of the reign of Jehoiakim king of Judah, Nebuchadnezzar king of Babylon came to Jerusalem and besieged it. And the Lord gave Jehoiakim king of Judah into his hand, with some of the vessels of the house of God. And he brought them to the land of Shinar, to the house of his god, and placed the vessels in the treasury of his god" (Dan. 1:1–2).

We can read this verse and blow right by it. But it is huge in biblical history, and it was huge for Daniel. When Nebuchadnezzar showed up at the gates of Jerusalem, it was the beginning of the end.

When I was a kid in school in the fifties, we used to have drills where we would duck under our desks in case of a nuclear attack from the Soviet Union. The Russian president, Khrushchev, had said he would bury us. So we got under our desks so that we would be protected from the Soviet nuclear missiles. That way Khrushchev couldn't bury us, and our nation wouldn't be crushed.

The prophet Jeremiah had told the nation that if they continued to rebel against the one true God and mock His Word, they would crash. And that's exactly what happened. Nebuchadnezzar showed up in 605 BC, and everything changed.

It would have been easy for Daniel to imagine that his life was over. God's judgment had arrived, and it was everyone's worst nightmare. Another king from a more powerful nation was now calling the shots. He would leave a Jewish king in place, but only as a figurehead and puppet. For the little nation of Judah, the gig was up.

When the nation crashed, so did Daniel's plan for his life. He was just a teenager, but teenagers have dreams, hopes, and wonderful ideas about what their lives will look like someday.

For Daniel, *that* someday—the someday of his boyhood dreams—would never come. All of those dreams died when the Babylonians smashed through Jerusalem's gates. All the rules had changed, and nothing could ever look or feel the same again. Not ever.

Sometimes our worlds crash, and so do our dreams.

I have a friend who waved to his wife and daughter as they drove off for a short overnight trip. Two hours later he was in a helicopter, landing at the scene of a head-on collision that took his wife's life and severely injured his daughter. When that truck crossed the center divider and crashed head-on into his wife's car, my friend's entire existence crashed. He held her lifeless body in his arms, and it was the end of everything—or so it seemed in that moment.

At some point every man's life crashes, and it seems like life is over. It may be the death of a spouse or a child. It could be the death of a marriage. A man's life can crash through a bankruptcy or because a teenager has run away from home. There are a thousand different events that can crash our lives. Sometimes the crash is the result of a bad decision, but it can just as easily be the result of simply living life.

When a man's life crashes, it always kicks in cause and effect.

Sometimes, the results are devastating, and a man simply gives up, withdraws in defeat and despair, and checks out of life. In other words, the crash changes everything—permanently, and for the worse. At other times, a man will take a different course and keep moving forward, trusting God, though the path has all but disappeared in front of him.

That, my friend, is a counterintuitive response.

And that is the path of True Courage.

The Change

Some changes are exciting, propelling you into a new and positive life. But when the change is the direct result of a crash, it's another matter altogether. Your life and your heart have been broken—and you're wondering how in the world you will ever pick up the pieces. You're in the middle of a transition, an unwanted change, and there's no turning back. And when you find yourself in unwelcome change, you are suddenly dealing with new stuff in your gut—anxiety, perplexity, disorientation, crushing disappointment, or even sheer terror.

The road forks before you, and you find yourself walking where you have never walked before. You wake up one morning, and it seems like everything once so dear and familiar to you has been stripped away. You're on alien turf and maybe wondering how in the world you got there—and what you're going to do next. And then you remember the crash and realize that's how you got there—but you still don't have a clue what you're going to do next.

Here's how the Bible describes the huge changes that crashed into the life of the young man named Daniel:

> Then the king commanded Ashpenaz, his chief eunuch, to bring some of the people of Israel, both of the royal family and of the nobility, youths without blemish, of good appearance and skillful in all wisdom, endowed with knowledge, understanding learning, and competent to stand in the king's palace, and to teach them the literature and language of the Chaldeans. The king assigned them a daily portion of the food that the king ate, and of the wine that he drank. They were to be educated for three years, and at the end of that time they were to stand before the king. Among these were Daniel, Hananiah, Mishael, and Azariah of the tribe of Judah. And the chief of the eunuchs gave them names: Daniel he called Belteshazzar, Hananiah he called Shadrach, Mishael he called Meshach, and Azariah he called Abednego. (Dan. 1:3–7)

Daniel's nation crashed, and so did his world. Almost overnight, he found himself swimming in unwanted change. He was taken from his family, friends, and home, and relocated to a foreign city, with a foreign culture, trying to pick up some basic phrases in a foreign language. And on top of that, he suddenly landed in a foreign university.

That's a lot of unwanted change—but that's what happens when your world comes crashing down. Daniel was immediately enrolled in a three-year course of study at the University of Babylon. You might call it Daniel's "education," but then again, the word *indoctrination* might fall closer to the mark. So what has changed? It's still true today. Indoctrination is still the primary work of secular universities, just as it was three thousand years ago in ancient Babylon.

If you think that I overstate the case, note that something had to occur before Daniel could move into the dorm. They first stripped him of his name—which was step one in stripping him of his faith. One commentator writes, "Daniel and his friends received genuine heathen names in exchange for their own significant names, which were associated with that of the true God."[1]

The Babylonian conquerors wanted to swallow these young people whole—mind, body, and soul—completely estranging them from their old home and their relationship with the God of Israel.

Daniel in Hebrew means "God is my Judge." It was changed to *Belteshazzar,* which means "whom Bel favors." Daniel's friends also went through the same drill. *Hananiah* means "God is gracious." He became known as *Shadrach,* which means "illumined by Shad [a sun god]." *Mishael* means "who is like God? God is great." They tagged him with *Meshach,* which means "who is like Shach [a love goddess]." Finally, *Azariah* means "God is my helper," but the tenured university faculty came up with *Abednego,* which means "the servant of Nego [a fire god]."[2]

Daniel found himself in a Babylonian university system that was a place of tremendous pressure and competition. At the end of the three years, each of the young men brought over from Judah were to stand before the king for the biggest final exam of their young lives. What's more, I'm pretty sure they couldn't bring their books, CliffsNotes, laptops, or iPhones to the exam. This is how Scripture records that moment after the university had dubbed Daniel and his friends with new names:

> Daniel resolved that he would not defile himself with the king's food, or with the wine that he drank. Therefore he asked the chief of the eunuchs to allow him not to defile himself. And God gave Daniel favor and compassion in the sight of the chief of the eunuchs, and the chief of the eunuchs said to Daniel, "I fear my lord the king, who assigned your food and your drink; for why should he see that you were in worse condition than the youths who are of your own age? So you would endanger my head with the king." Then Daniel said to the steward whom the chief of the eunuchs had assigned over Daniel, Hananiah, Mishael, and Azariah, "Test your servants for ten days; let us be given vegetables to eat and water to drink. Then let our appearance and the appearance of the youths who eat the king's food be observed by you, and deal with your servants according to what you see." So he listened to them in this matter, and tested them for ten days. At the end of ten days it was seen that they were better in appearance and fatter in flesh than all the youths who ate the king's food. So the steward took

away their food and the wine they were to drink,
and gave them vegetables.

As for these four youths, God gave them
learning and skill in all literature and wisdom,
and Daniel had understanding in all visions and
dreams. At the end of the time, when the king
had commanded that they should be brought in,
the chief of the eunuchs brought them in before
Nebuchadnezzar. And the king spoke with them,
and among all of them none was found like Daniel,
Hananiah, Mishael, and Azariah. Therefore they
stood before the king. And in every matter of
wisdom and understanding about which the king
inquired of them, he found them ten times better
than all the magicians and enchanters that were in
all his kingdom. And Daniel was there until the
first year of King Cyrus. (Dan. 1:8–21)

In Daniel 1:3, Daniel was a teenager. By the time we reach verse
21, he's somewhere around ninety years of age. Cyrus conquered
Babylon in 539 BC. Verses 3–21 give us a very short bio of Daniel's
career in Babylon. He started in the Babylonian university, was promoted like a rocket, and served in the highest reaches of power for at
least seventy years.

In the early years at that godless university, God prepared Daniel
and his sidekicks to serve as royal advisors to the king of Babylon.
In addition, God gave Daniel a stunning gift: the ability to interpret
dreams and visions. He was truly one of a kind. He and his friends

who stood for the Lord had a place of remarkable influence because their advice, counsel, and wisdom were ten times better than anyone who had ever graduated from the University of Babylon.

At the risk of their very lives, these young men honored God by refusing to violate their consciences, and the Lord honored their faithfulness. Daniel went on to keep his high place of honor for *seventy years*. For the rest of his life he would live and work in the corridors of power and luxury, politics, and intrigue. The king and the palace were to be his sphere for the rest of his days.

Now how in the world did he do that?

THREE TRAITS

How did this young man maintain his balance on such treacherous turf? And did he manage to keep that balance for the seventy years of his life there?

As I have read and reread the account of Daniel's life, three traits continually come to the surface: humility, trust, and hope.

They don't show up just once or twice. Throughout his life they are woven into the fabric of his character and decision making. They are a key part of Daniel's True Courage. That may not seem obvious at first glance—what does humility, trust, and hope have to do with True Courage? The answer is all three are counterintuitive. They all run against the grain of what we would expect in Daniel.

It hit me one day that those three traits in Daniel's life are captured in one of the shortest psalms in the Bible: Psalm 131. Interestingly enough, it's one of the psalms of the ascent—psalms that the men of Judah would sing as they would make their way up the mountain to Jerusalem three times a year. God commanded all of the men to come during these times. But Daniel was never able to do that in his entire life. The nation was in captivity, and the feasts were on hold.

But the traits of Psalm 131 weren't on hold in his life.

He lived them out every day and in so doing demonstrated True Courage.

He actually lived out that psalm's truths in a sometimes seductive, always tyrannical environment. And he did it for seventy years.

It was C. H. Spurgeon who commented that Psalm 131 is one of the shortest psalms to read … and one of the longest to learn.

> O Lord, my heart is not lifted up;
>> my eyes are not raised too high;
>
> I do not occupy myself with things
>> too great and too marvelous for me.
>
> But I have calmed and quieted my soul,
>> like a weaned child with its mother;
>> like a weaned child is my soul within me.
>> O Israel, hope in the Lord
>> from this time forth and forevermore. (Ps. 131:1–3)

Did you catch the three essential traits in this psalm? Verse 1 speaks of the trait of humility. Verse 2 focuses on trust, and verse 3 speaks of a great hope. It's safe to say that Daniel consistently exhibited these traits throughout his life.

ESSENTIAL TRAIT 1: HUMILITY

If you're out looking for an example of humility, you probably shouldn't start with the NFL—and particularly with wide receivers. Wide receivers, generally speaking, are known for their arrogant touchdown dances. There are notable exceptions, but arrogance could be tattooed quite naturally on most of them.

It seems like whenever these guys just happen to catch a pass in the end zone, they suddenly start pounding their chests and strutting around like a peacock. Now what's ironic is that the guy probably dropped the last four balls that were thrown his way. But this one he caught because it went through his hands and lodged in his face mask. So now he's running around like he just did something important. What he did was catch a football. He's paid (actually overpaid) to catch footballs.

The wide receiver who catches a touchdown pass and then offers a sacrifice to the god of self in the end zone has forgotten a few things. He has forgotten that the touchdown was actually a team effort. There was a quarterback who had the guts to stand in the pocket and get sandwiched by six hundred pounds of blitzing wild men. There are also the anonymous offensive linemen who do the work in the trenches that nobody sees or appreciates. They get stepped on, kicked in the groin, and blinded by a thumb in the eyes. And that's just during pregame warm-ups! Arrogance is getting full of yourself real quick and losing all perspective concerning your accomplishments.

There are two ways we can depart from humility. The first is arrogance, and it's also been known to show up in individuals who are not wide receivers. (Frankly, you can be an incredibly arrogant person at a fast-food counter. I've met some of them.) Verse 1 is a description of balanced humility. The psalmist says that his heart is not lifted up. He's not saying that his heart has *never* been lifted up, but rather that he's trying to keep his heart in check. In other words, David is doing a little self-assessment here. He's checking out his heart, as Solomon advised in Proverbs 4:23: "Keep your heart with all vigilance, for from it flow the springs of life."

The psalmist then makes sure his eyes aren't raised too high so that they're not too lofty. In other words, he's careful of putting all of his energy into reaching the next level—whatever that may be. "There is nothing wrong with the desire to do well," wrote D. Martyn Lloyd-Jones, "as long as it does not master us. We must not be governed by ambition."[3]

The writer knows that it is God who grants promotion (Ps. 75), and He knows best when we are ready for the higher place. Until then, we should mind our assigned posts—and ourselves.

Humility doesn't try to understand things that are beyond comprehension. Humility understands that some answers to hard questions will remain secret (Deut. 29:29). And that's okay.

The second way we can wander away from humility is when we get into self-condemnation and self-loathing. We do something stupid that we promised ourselves we would never do again—and then because of our disappointment, we start telling ourselves we're worthless. We've all done stupid things—and then done them again and again.

Speaking for myself, I've got enough hours in "stupid" to get a PhD. I actually have enough hours in "stupid" to teach "stupid" at a graduate level. And if we have really screwed up and done something that has horrible consequences—not only for us but also for the people we love—we start riding ourselves and telling ourselves that it would be better for them if we weren't even alive.

Whenever a believer commits suicide, you must suspect that there was demonic oppression involved, which led to self-condemnation and self-loathing. That's the work of Satan. The Bible doesn't call him the "accuser of the brethren" for nothing.

So what is humility and how do we find its balance that keeps us from arrogance on one hand and self-condemnation on the other? C. J. Mahaney hit the nail on the head when he stated, "Humility is honestly assessing ourselves in light of God's holiness and our sinfulness."[4] Romans 12:3–8 really brings it into focus:

> For by the grace given to me I say to everyone among you not to think of himself more highly than he ought to think, but to think with sober judgment, each according to the measure of faith that God has assigned. For as in one body we have many members, and the members do not all have the same function, so we, though many, are one body in Christ, and individually members one of another. Having gifts that differ according to the grace given to us, let us use them: if

prophecy, in proportion to our faith; if service,
in our serving; the one who teaches, in his teaching; the one who exhorts, in his exhortation; the
one who contributes, in generosity; the one who
leads, with zeal; the one who does acts of mercy,
with cheerfulness.

I see three principles here that helped Daniel keep his balance
with humility and that I believe will help us do the same.

- Know who you are
- Know what God has given to you
- Stay in your sphere

How to Keep Your Balance
Know Who You Are

The plumb line on humility is this: Don't think too highly of
yourself—and don't think too lowly, either.

I like the way J. B. Phillips paraphrased Romans 12:3:

As your spiritual teacher I give this piece of advice
to each one of you. Don't cherish exaggerated ideas
of yourself or your importance, but try to have a
sane estimate of your capabilities by the light of the
faith that God has given to you all.

This passage directs us to use sober or sound judgment (or "a sane estimate") in knowing who you are. If you're an average singer, don't plan on cutting a CD and taking a worldwide tour. You may like music, and your brother-in-law might think you're pretty good at karaoke, but if you're average or even a little above average, chances are you're not going to make it in New York or Nashville.

Know What God Has Given You

You don't have all of the gifts mentioned in Romans 12:3–8. You're part of the body of Christ, and He has distributed gifts to each of us. Some have more gifts than others—but everyone has a gift.

We often meet someone whom we respect and admire and think, *I wish I could be like him,* or maybe, *I wish I had his personality.* But you can't be like him, and you don't have his personality. That individual may have gifts you don't have, but don't waste your time—and your life—moping around because you don't have certain gifts. When you do that, your heart is getting proud, your eyes are getting lofty, and you're not thinking straight. What are the gifts God has given to *you?* Don't depreciate them, and don't despise them. And don't imagine that they're not important—to God and to others.

Years ago I was up early on a Sunday morning and discovered we were out of something—salt, sugar, Ovaltine—I honestly can't remember what it was. It was too many years ago. But here's what I do remember. I found what I was looking for on the top shelf of the pantry, and when I reached up to grab it, I knocked over a glass jar of

sweet pickles that immediately yielded to the law of gravity and fell
seven feet where it landed on my unprotected pinkie toe.

I'd never given much thought to my pinkie toe and its ministry
in my life until that moment. But for the next three or four months I
had trouble thinking about anything else. When that pickle-assaulted
pinkie toe was broken, it messed up my entire life. I couldn't walk,
I couldn't sleep, and I couldn't think. I just wanted that little toe to
heal up and get back to its assigned post.

Stay in Your Sphere

You've been given gifts. Stay with them. Develop them, work
hard, and do your work to the glory of God. Colossians 3:23–24 says,
"Whatever you do, do your work heartily, as for the Lord rather than
for men, knowing that from the Lord you will receive the reward of
the inheritance. It is the Lord Christ whom you serve" (NASB).

All work is valuable, and even the Babylonian heathens knew
this when they took over Jerusalem and brought back the first round
of exiles. In Jeremiah 29:1–2, the prophet makes reference to the
people who were taken in the second wave from Judah to Babylon
in 597 BC:

> These are the words of the letter that Jeremiah
> the prophet sent from Jerusalem to the surviving
> elders of the exiles, and to the priests, the prophets,
> and all the people, whom Nebuchadnezzar had
> taken into exile from Jerusalem to Babylon. This
> was after King Jeconiah and the queen mother, the

eunuchs, the officials of Judah and Jerusalem, the craftsmen, and the metal workers had departed from Jerusalem.

Daniel and his buddies were members of the educated royal family and had already been taken and enrolled in the University of Babylon (Dan. 1:1–7). But in the second wave, the Babylonians brought back additional members of the royal family, some government bureaucrats, and, watch this—craftsmen and metal workers.

You can understand their bringing in the government guys and the queen, but why would they single out craftsmen and metal workers? It was because they were valuable. Guys who are gifted with their hands, who can work with wood or metal, are critical. Try to build an army without craftsmen and metal workers. Those are the guys who build the chariots and the siege ramps and supply the infantry with swords and armor.

If you're gifted with your hands—if you're a finish carpenter or an excellent craftsman—don't waste your time wishing you could be a preacher or a prime minister. That's not your calling, and it's not your sphere. Work with that wood, excel with that needle and thread, and do it to the glory of God!

On the other hand, Daniel, who was gifted with the wisdom and knowledge to lead a government, should not have been shoeing horses and working around a forge. That is honorable and critical work, but Daniel wasn't called or gifted in that area. He needed to stay in his sphere. He wasn't to think too highly or too lowly of himself. Instead, he correctly assessed his own gifts and then got after it with what God had given him.

Staying in your sphere doesn't mean that you don't improve yourself—you do. So take some classes and get the credentials you need to succeed in your sphere. That may mean that you need a college degree—but then again, you may not need a college degree if you're going to repair cars or make crowns in a dental lab. But whatever your sphere is, work hard, show up on time, better yourself, do quality work, and God will see to your advancement. But don't try to be something that you're not!

Right off the top, I'm reminded of a king in the Old Testament who refused to stay in his sphere: Uzziah, king of Judah.

Uzziah started strong. He was one of the most productive kings that Judah ever had. His vast accomplishments are listed in 2 Chronicles 26:14. And then we read these words:

> In Jerusalem he made engines, invented by skill-
> ful men, to be on the towers and the corners,
> to shoot arrows and great stones. And his fame
> spread far, for he was marvelously helped, till he
> was strong.
>
> But when he was strong, he grew proud, to his
> destruction. For he was unfaithful to the LORD his
> God and entered the temple of the LORD to burn
> incense on the altar of incense. But Azariah the priest
> went in after him, with eighty priests of the LORD
> who were men of valor, and they withstood King
> Uzziah and said to him, "It is not for you, Uzziah,
> to burn incense to the LORD, but for the priests, the
> sons of Aaron, who are consecrated to burn incense.

Go out of the sanctuary, for you have done wrong, and it will bring you no honor from the LORD God." Then Uzziah was angry. Now he had a censer in his hand to burn incense, and when he became angry with the priests, leprosy broke out on his forehead in the presence of the priests in the house of the LORD, by the altar of incense. And Azariah the chief priest and all the priests looked at him, and behold, he was leprous in his forehead! And they rushed him out quickly, and he himself hurried to go out, because the LORD had struck him. And King Uzziah was a leper to the day of his death, and being a leper lived in a separate house, for he was excluded from the house of the LORD. And Jotham his son was over the king's household, governing the people of the land. (2 Chron. 26:15–21)

What haunting words: *"He was marvelously helped, till he was strong."*

When he became strong, he grew proud and lost his humility. And it led to his destruction. He refused to stay in his sphere and decided that he would go ahead and do the work that was only to be done by the priest. When he lost his humility, he refused to stay in his sphere—and he was disciplined as a leper for the rest of his days. Then he was *forced* to stay in his sphere—in a separate house, excluded from the house of the Lord.

Daniel was humble enough to stay in his sphere.

And God favored his life and work for the next seventy years.

ESSENTIAL TRAIT 2: TRUST

The second essential trait is trust in God, and it's something that takes years to learn. We fight it from the time we are born as Psalm 131:2 describes: "But I have calmed and quieted my soul, like a weaned child with its mother; like a weaned child is my soul within me."

In the days of the Old Testament, children often weren't weaned until the age of three or four. And when the day of weaning came, the little ones fought against it with everything within them. The mother's breast was the place of security, comfort, affection, and nourishment. But a child must get on with life, and so the time of weaning comes.

Weaning is the first great disappointment of life.

No matter what our age, however, God is continually weaning us from places or positions where we have found comfort, peace, security, nourishment, or affirmation. Sometimes we fight with everything we have to maintain those places of safety, comfort, and security—especially if it involves our income stream.

The mother's milk is the source of provision, and no child wants to lose it. The sudden loss of a secure and consistent income scares us and makes us worry about our future. A job loss brings anxiety as we suddenly have to calibrate how we'll buy groceries and pay the mortgage. When we lose a job or we lose our health—we're being weaned, and it isn't pleasant. And so we are forced into the place of trust.

Elijah the prophet confronted King Ahab and his wife, Jezebel, telling them that because of their Baal worship and their belief that Baal controlled the rain, it would not rain until God's drought would run its course (1 Kings 17). It turned out to be a three-and-half-year drought. Immediately Elijah became number one on Israel's most-wanted list. God, however, led him to a strange and unfamiliar refuge east of the Jordan, hiding him by a brook called Cherith.

Elijah had suddenly been weaned off his home, his income, and his security. Now he was in a secluded place where the economic outlook wasn't good. Without much time to adapt, he found himself having to trust God to give him the daily essentials of life. He had no IRAs to cash in or gold to get him through the crisis. As far as I know, Old Testament prophets didn't get a pension from the government or have 401(k) accounts.

But he had the Lord, and He is always enough.

During Elijah's time of exile, he'd had fresh water from the bubbling brook, and each morning God would send the ravens with his brunch—and then they would return that evening with dinner. He had no reserves and no savings. He had to trust God—literally—to give him this day his daily bread. And God strangely chose to use the ravens—which are notorious for neglecting to feed their own young. But they never forgot Elijah. This wasn't meals on wheels; it was dinner on the fly!

After awhile he began to feel comfortable and secure. He was adjusting nicely to his new circumstances. And then one morning the brook went dry.

Once again he was in crisis. He was being weaned off the familiar and the secure. His source of provision suddenly dried up, and now he was going to have to trust God all over again.

> Then the word of the LORD came to him, "Arise, go
> to Zarephath, which belongs to Sidon, and dwell

there. Behold, I have commanded a widow there
to feed you." So he arose and went to Zarephath.
And when he came to the gate of the city, behold,
a widow was there gathering sticks. And he called
to her and said, "Bring me a little water in a vessel,
that I may drink." And as she was going to bring
it, he called to her and said, "Bring me a morsel
of bread in your hand." And she said, "As the
LORD your God lives, I have nothing baked, only
a handful of flour in a jar and a little oil in a jug.
And now I am gathering a couple of sticks that I
may go in and prepare it for myself and my son,
that we may eat it and die." And Elijah said to her,
"Do not fear; go and do as you have said. But first
make me a little cake of it and bring it to me, and
afterward make something for yourself and your
son. For thus says the LORD, the God of Israel,
'The jar of flour shall not be spent, and the jug of
oil shall not be empty, until the day that the LORD
sends rain upon the earth.'" And she went and did
as Elijah said. And she and he and her household
ate for many days. The jar of flour was not spent,
neither did the jug of oil become empty, according
to the word of the LORD that he spoke by Elijah.
(1 Kings 17:8–16)

So Elijah must have been thinking that this widow up in
Zarephath had a foundation from the life-insurance money her

husband had left. But when he arrived, he found out that she was in worse shape than he was. He asked her for a blueberry waffle, and she replied that she was going to make one for her and her boy, and then they were going to die. But she agreed to feed Elijah first—and then a convoy of large trucks immediately began to pull up in front of her house with thousands of gallons of Crisco oil and one-hundred-pound sacks of Gold Medal flour. She quickly hired workers to construct large warehouses to hold her great surplus of flour and vegetable oil.

No, that's not quite how it happened, is it?

In fact, she just kept working out of the same jar of flour and the same jug of oil. She would reach in and dip out a cup of oil, and when she did, the level never dropped—and it was the same with the flour.

She didn't have a three-year supply down in the root cellar. There never was a surplus—God just made sure that she always had enough to get by. And when that happens, you are forced to trust Him on a daily basis. When you get down to it, that's not a bad way to live. It keeps us connected with our Provider and mindful that we can't take a step or a breath without Him.

And that leads to the next essential trait.

ESSENTIAL TRAIT 3: HOPE

Over the last year I have come to a startling realization.

It's simply this: The greatest blessings of my life have all come out of my greatest disappointments. I won't bore you with the details, but every time I thought I was done or found myself fighting off some crushing setback—God brought along a blessing far greater than I could have asked for or imagined. Those disappointments have been a series of weanings. I had to be weaned off what I wanted and what I had prescribed for my own life. Eventually I would quit fighting the loss of what I wanted to happen and simply trust that He knew what was best. And that has always proven to be the case.

That's how it worked for Daniel. He was humbled when his nation was taken over by Babylon, and no doubt he had to be weaned off his family and friends who were back in Jerusalem. Through it all, however, he learned to hope in the God of Israel who never slumbers or sleeps.

That's our story too, as we go through life. We are humbled by some crushing setback, great failure, or defeat. We find ourselves getting weaned off something that we dearly love and want to hold on to. Through the humiliations and weanings, however, we learn that God will never abandon us. He may not give us what we want, but He always gives us what we need. And what He gives is always infinitely better than we could have ever thought or imagined— and that in turn builds our hope when the next hard and difficult time comes ripping and ramming into our lives like a runaway bulldozer.

The bottom line is this: Daniel's hope was completely in God. That's it. That's the Christian life.

Do you find yourself in a humiliating defeat? Are you being weaned off something that you are trying to hold on to?

Let it go. Submit yourself to Him and to His plan for your life. That's what Daniel did. Trust him with everything. You will find that it's the safest and most secure place in the entire world.

Stay in your sphere—and trust the God who isn't bound by spheres.

In the process, you'll find True Courage.

"We are all imprisoned by facts:
I was born, I exist."

Luigi Pirandello

Chapter Two

ACTS AND FACTS

Courage shows itself best in tight places.

God's men often find themselves in tight places. The problem with a tight place is that if you make the wrong move, you're finished. And sometimes the tight place is so narrow and confined that you can't move at all.

In Psalm 46:1, David writes:

> God is our refuge and strength,
> a very present help in trouble.

Giving the sense of the kind of help we can expect from God, a marginal note in *The English Standard Version* indicates that His help is "well-proved." *The New American Standard Bible* note brings out an even stronger sense of help, noting, "He is abundantly available for help in tight places." So let's put those two ideas together:

God is our refuge and strength,
He is well proved to be abundantly available in tight
    places.

So if you find yourself right now in an incredibly tight place, or if you're concerned that such a place awaits you in your future, know this: Your God and Savior is well proved to be abundantly available for help in tight places.

- Daniel was in a tight place at the Babylonian cafeteria.
- David was in a tight place in the cave.
- Churchill was in a tight place when he stepped into the role of wartime prime minister and it looked like England had no hope of victory.
- I was in a tight place at the Miami airport in 1966—and the circumstances seemed so overwhelming I saw no possible solution.

When you find yourself in a tight place and it looks like there's no possible way out, there are two things you must possess in order to keep steady and not lose heart.

You need acts, and you need facts.

Christianity is all about facts. It's all about truth. Harry Blamires, in his brilliant book *The Christian Mind*, capsulizes what Daniel believed and what every modern-day Christian should believe:

The Christian faith is important because it is true
... to think Christianly is to think in terms of

Revelation. For the secularist, God and theology are the playthings of the mind. For the Christian, God is real, and Christian theology describes his truth revealed to us. For the secular mind, religion is essentially a matter of theory: for the Christian mind, Christianity is a matter of acts and facts. The acts and facts which are the basis of our faith are recorded in the Bible. They have been interpreted and illuminated in the long history of the Church. The Christian mind is inescapably and unbrokenly conscious of the hard, factual quality of the Christian Faith.... For Christianity is so much more than a mere moral code, a recipe of virtue, a system of comfortable idealistic thought. It is a religion of acts and facts. Its God is not an abstraction, but a Person—with a right arm and voice. Its God has moved among us. *How wonderful are Thy works!*[1]

The works of God are the acts of God. He can do fabulous acts because He has unlimited power. "Is anything too hard for the Lord?" Of course not. So what do you do when the tight place threatens to choke off your very existence? You live off the facts—facts that cannot be refuted or challenged. We have a God who acts. And if He has acted in the past, why wouldn't He act now?

DANIEL'S TIGHT PLACE

God plays kings and political leaders like a Steinway piano. That's a fact. And although the king of Babylon had come to Jerusalem and disrupted the life of Daniel and his nation, that king was marching to God's tune. When the Babylonian special forces showed up on his doorstep, Daniel suddenly underwent a major transfer in his higher education.

Some college athletes transfer to another college in order to get more playing time. Daniel and his friends didn't have the opportunity to play college ball. But they did transfer schools. Only, it wasn't a decision of their own making. As members of the royal family and nobles, they had the very best of education at the University of Jerusalem. But then they found themselves transferring to the University of Babylon. Their families, their hopes, their dreams, their plans, and their careers were suddenly devastated and destroyed by that radical upheaval in their lives. As a result, they weren't looking for more playing time … but there's no doubt they were getting in a lot more praying time.

Almost from the beginning of their lives in Babylon, they found themselves in a very tight place—and it began when Daniel respectfully yet firmly refused to defile himself with the royal Babylonian cuisine. We don't know all of the details, but it's abundantly clear that his conscience would not allow him to eat what was being offered.

Every sensible person in that day knew very well that you just don't say no to the all-powerful king of the Babylonian Empire.

Or do you?

The tight place is described in Daniel 1:8–14:

But Daniel resolved that he would not defile himself with the king's food, or with the wine that he drank. Therefore he asked the chief of the eunuchs to allow him not to defile himself. And God gave Daniel favor and compassion in the sight of the chief of the eunuchs, and the chief of the eunuchs said to Daniel, "I fear my lord the king, who assigned your food and your drink; for why should he see that you were in worse condition than the youths who are of your own age? So you would endanger my head with the king." Then Daniel said to the steward whom the chief of the eunuchs had assigned over Daniel, Hananiah, Mishael, and Azariah, "Test your servants for ten days; let us be given vegetables to eat and water to drink. Then let our appearance and the appearance of the youths who eat the king's food be observed by you, and deal with your servants according to what you see." So he listened to them in this matter, and tested them for ten days.

It's very clear that Daniel had a remarkable understanding of the greatness and majesty of God. Daniel believed certain things about the existence and activities of the God of Israel. In other words, he lived off certain facts.

This describes Daniel's approach to living throughout his entire book. And we first see it in this initial crisis over the Babylonian diet, which Daniel and his sidekicks couldn't go along with. Because he believed that God was a person and that God was holy—those are facts—he could not violate his conscience and sin against God. So what did he do?

- He opted out (v. 8).
- He offered an option (vv. 9–13).
- He overcame the objection (vv. 14–16).
- He outdistanced the others (vv. 17–20).

> At the end of ten days it was seen that they were better in appearance and fatter in flesh than all the youths who ate the king's food. So the steward took away their food and the wine they were to drink, and gave them vegetables.
>
> As for these four youths, God gave them learning and skill in all literature and wisdom, and Daniel had understanding in all visions and dreams. At the end of the time, when the king had commanded that they should be brought in, the chief of the eunuchs brought them in before Nebuchadnezzar. And the king spoke with them, and among all of them none was found like Daniel, Hananiah, Mishael, and Azariah. Therefore they stood before the king. And in every matter of wisdom and understanding about which the king inquired of them, he found them ten times better than all the magicians and enchanters that were

in all his kingdom. And Daniel was there until the
first year of King Cyrus. (vv. 15–21)

FACT: Daniel believed that his destiny was in the hands of God.
By taking the stand that he did, he could have very well displeased the king. And to upset a Babylonian king is a high-risk game. But it was a stand that Daniel was willing to take, even if it cost him his young life. Now how could he take such a stand in such a tight place? Where did he find such courage at a young age?

It all started with facts Daniel believed concerning his God. These were facts he had undoubtedly gripped from his earliest memory.

Daniel believed in God's sovereignty over times and events. The message of the entire book of Daniel shouts the fact that God is in absolute control and that the rulers and people of the earth are all passing away. That's why Daniel and his friends stood tall against tyranny whenever their lives were threatened. They believed acts and facts. They believed certain facts about God and they believed that this same God was a God who acts.

Blamires drives home the point:

> A prime mark of the Christian mind is that it
> cultivates the eternal perspective. That is to say,
> it looks beyond this life to another one. It is
> supernaturally oriented, and brings to bear upon
> earthly considerations the fact of Heaven and the
> fact of Hell.[2]

That's the message of the book of Daniel. It looks beyond this life to another. It is supernaturally oriented because of the fact that God exists.

It was the will of God that they were shifted from Jerusalem. If it wasn't God's purpose and plan for them, it never would have happened. Daniel stated in 2:21 that it is God who "changes the times and the seasons" (NKJV). It was God who changed the season of their lives. He was the one who had moved them from Jerusalem to Babylon. That was a *fact* to them. It was by God's design and destiny that they were in Babylon—and that they were in a tight place in regard to the issue of diet.

Ephesians 1:11 declares that truth: "In him we have obtained an inheritance, having been predestined according to the purpose of him who works all things according to the counsel of his will."

God doesn't work some things according to the counsel of His will—He works *all* things. It's evident throughout the entire book of Daniel that Daniel and his friends believed that truth.

And staked their very lives on it.

DAVID'S TIGHT PLACE

Psalm 57 and Psalm 142 are known as the "cave" psalms. The inscriptions at the beginning of each of these psalms tell us that David wrote them when he was running for his life—and he was holed up in a cave.

What were his chances? When you're hiding in a cave in a small country with a whole army trying to nail your hide to the wall, your chances of survival are pretty slim.

David had been anointed to replace Saul as king of Israel. Because of Saul's continual disobedience, however, God had decided to hand the throne to David, a young shepherd from the hills of Judah. Knowing this, the jealous king began an insane pursuit to keep that from happening, instituting the greatest manhunt in the history of Israel. The son of Jesse's mug shot was in every post office in Israel. He couldn't go near a town without fear of being caught and handed over. As the months and years dragged on, Saul continued to cinch the net tighter and tighter around David's escape routes. It got so bad that the only place of safety David could find was a cave.

Ultimately David was delivered from Saul's manhunt. But before he was freed, when he was in the dark, dank recesses of the cave, what sustained him were the acts and facts relating to his God. Note Psalm 57:2–3:

> I will cry to God Most High,
>   To God who accomplishes all things for me.
> He will send from heaven and save me. (NASB)

In the other cave psalm, once again, David is chewing—not on kibbles and bits, but on acts and facts:

> When my spirit was overwhelmed within me,
>   You knew my path. (Ps. 142:3 NASB)

FACT: David believed that his destiny was in the hands of God.
That's how you endure in the cave.
That's how you survive the tight place.

CHURCHILL'S TIGHT PLACE

Paul Johnson wrote that "of all the towering figures of the twentieth century, both good and evil, Winston Churchill was the most valuable to humanity, and also the most likable."[3] To prove the point, consider a very unique bookstore near Rockefeller Center in New York City. We all know that there are many fine bookstores in New York City, but Chartwell's stands out as an establishment that carries books only by, or about, one man: Winston Churchill. Chartwell's advertises themselves as the world's only Winston Churchill bookshop. The masthead on the website sums it all up:

"Winston Churchill First Editions. Signed Books by Winston Churchill. Rare Books by Winston Churchill. Books About Winston Churchill. Churchill Speeches. Churchill Paintings. Churchill photographs. Churchilliana."[4]

Even with all of that information available at Chartwell's about Winston Churchill, there's a fact that might get overlooked:

FACT: Winston Churchill believed that his destiny was in the hands of God.

When Churchill was finally appointed as prime minister in the early days of World War II, England was like a punch-drunk fighter on the ropes, and Germany was on the rise. Circumstances looked bleak for England, and many thought they were already defeated. And it was in that context that Churchill came in as prime minister. The situation seemed incredibly dark, with no identifiable light at the end of the tunnel. Here's how Churchill himself described the momentous day he took office:

Thus at the outset of this mighty battle, I acquired the chief power in the State.... As I went to bed about 3 a.m., I was conscious of a profound sense of relief. At last I had the authority to give directions over the whole scene. I felt as if I were walking with destiny, and that all my past life had been but a preparation for this hour and for this trial. Eleven years in the political wilderness had freed me from ordinary Party antagonisms. My warnings over the last six years had been so numerous, so detailed, and were now so terribly vindicated, that no one could gainsay me. I could not be reproached either for making the war or with want of preparation for it.... Therefore, although impatient for the morning, I slept soundly and had no need for cheering dreams. Facts are better than dreams.[5]

"Facts are better than dreams."

Churchill believed as fact that God had a destiny for his life. And in the midst of all hell breaking out around him by Hitler's conquering army, navy, and Luftwaffe, Churchill went to bed and slept like a baby. How in the world could he do that? It's actually quite simple. He believed in the fact that God existed and had a plan for the world. He could go to sleep in the face of horrific odds against survival, let alone victory, because he believed as a fact that God had prepared him all of his life for that very moment.

Was Churchill a committed Christian who was in church every Sunday? No, he wasn't. In fact, he once said of himself, "I am not a pillar of the church but a buttress—I support it from the outside."[6]

Even so, Churchill knew his Bible. As a young boy he had been steeped in the Scriptures by his nanny, Mrs. Everest (whom he affectionately addressed as "Woom"), a wonderful Christian woman who loved Christ. She gave him a solid biblical foundation in his early years. As a result, when he was thirteen and a student at Harrow, "he came at the top in history, ancient history, Bible history, algebra.... He would win prizes for English and Scripture by the end of the year."[7]

At the top of his class in Bible history and Scripture, Churchill knew the facts about God. On another occasion during the war, he was scheduled to meet with President Franklin D. Roosevelt and Joseph Stalin in Cairo. FDR cabled his concern that the meeting place in Cairo could be easily bombed and perhaps the location should be changed. Churchill replied in nine words:

"See St. John, chapter 14, verses 1 to 4."[8]

FDR had to send an aid to find a Bible. And when he turned to John 14:1–4, he found not only Churchill's reply but also the words of the Lord Jesus Christ:

> Let not your hearts be troubled. Believe in God; believe also in me. In my Father's house are many rooms. If it were not so, would I have told you that I go to prepare a place for you? And if I go and prepare a place for you, I will come again and will take you to myself, that where I am you may be also. And you know the way to where I am going.

Churchill could not only sleep well as he faced a demonic invasion of Nazis, but he could also sign off on the location of a key meeting, in spite of the threat of bombing. Why? He believed in certain facts about God and the Lord Jesus, as outlined in John 14. Perhaps it would be more accurate to say that he was aware of the acts and facts in John 14.

In his book *Just As I Am*, Billy Graham chronicled a remarkable encounter with Churchill in 1954, just as Graham was ending his London crusade and heading for Scotland. Graham received a call from Prime Minister Churchill's secretary, inviting him to join Mr. Churchill for lunch the next day. Graham had to decline, since he was leaving for Scotland. Thirty minutes later the phone rang and the secretary asked if Graham could meet with Mr. Churchill at noon on that very day.

> When I arrived at Number 10 Downing Street, I was reminded discreetly by Mr. Colville [Churchill's secretary] that the prime minister had precisely twenty minutes....
>
> [Churchill asked,] "Tell me, Reverend Graham, what is it that filled Harringay night after night?"
>
> "I think it's the Gospel of Christ," I told him without hesitation. "People are hungry to hear a word straight from the Bible. Almost all the clergy of this country used to preach it faithfully, but I believe they have gotten away from it." ...
>
> "Yes," he said, sighing. "Things have changed tremendously. Look at these newspapers—filled

with nothing but murder and war and what the Communists are up to. You know, the world may one day be taken over by the Communists." ...

"Things do look dark," I agreed.... We talked at length about the world situation, and then, as if on cue, the prime minister looked me in the eye. "I am a man without hope," he said somberly. "Do you have any real hope?"

He might have been talking geopolitically, but to me this sounded like a personal plea....

"Are you without hope for your own soul's salvation?"

"Frankly, I think about that a great deal," he replied.

I had my New Testament with me. Knowing that we had but a few minutes left, I immediately explained the way of salvation. I watched carefully for signs of irritation or offense, but he seemed receptive, if not enthusiastic. I also talked about God's plan for the future, including the return of Christ. His eyes seemed to light up at the prospect.

At precisely twelve-thirty, Mr. Colville knocked. "Sir Winston, the Duke of Windsor is here for your luncheon," he said.

"Let him wait!" Mr. Churchill growled, waving Mr. Colville off and turning back to me. "Go ahead."[9]

And with that, Billy Graham went on explaining the gospel of Jesus Christ to one of the greatest leaders of the Free World. Although acclaimed by that world, Churchill was without peace or hope in his heart. I find it interesting that Churchill was so interested in the acts and facts concerning salvation that he told the Duke of Windsor to wait. The Duke of Windsor was the former king of England. No one told him to wait. But Churchill did, as he wanted Graham to finish the acts and facts about trusting in Christ alone for salvation. Churchill was in such a desperate place—such a tight place without any hope—that he made a human king wait while he found out the acts and facts about the King of Kings.

Churchill knew that facts were better than dreams. He couldn't face eternity living off in some sentimental dream. He needed the facts about eternal life.

RED LEATHER CHAIR, BLACK LEATHER BIBLE

Every university—whether in Jerusalem or Babylon, Boston or Los Angeles—has a library. It was Thomas Watson who said, "The Scriptures are the library of the Holy Ghost.... The Scriptures contain in it the *credenda*, 'the things which we are to believe,' and the *agenda*, 'the things which we are to practice.'"

I need to make sure I visit that library every day.

Recently I had breakfast with a young pastor who asked me, "How do you live your life?" I had never been asked that before, and I asked him to clarify it. "Well, you're here this weekend doing a men's conference. You travel quite a bit, and you teach a couple of men's studies in Dallas. And you write books. How do you do that? How do you do what you do and stay on track?"

I thought for a minute and said, "I live my life out of a red leather chair with a black leather Bible." And then I explained to him that I actually have a pretty set schedule. I get up in the morning, get a cup of coffee, get out my black leather Bible, and sit down in my red leather chair. For years I have followed Robert Murray M'Cheyne's Bible-reading calendar.[10] That calendar has me reading four chapters a day from four different books of the Bible. I consider it my morning briefing with my Commander in Chief.

I settle into my red leather chair with my black leather Bible most every morning. It's the cockpit of my life. Sinking back into my chair, I get a little coffee (or iced tea in the summer) flowing through my veins, and I check in with the Lord. I learned from my dad the importance of starting the day with the Word of God. He did it every day for over fifty years, and that's how he lived his life. He finished strong, and I want to finish strong.

I try to do that every morning because I need to recalibrate myself daily. I need to be reminded about who God is and what He says to me. I need to remember once again that He runs the world and that all the events in the news are moving according to His prophetic timetable and plan for the ages. And every morning His plan for the world and eternity is right on schedule. Therefore ... so is my life. No matter how events might stack up on any given morning, things aren't out of control, they are *under* control. His control.

Those are the acts and facts of my life.

The Scriptures are the library of the Holy Spirit. The Bible is true and therefore contains facts. Because these facts are true, we are to believe them and put those truths into practice. In other words, we are to live out and apply the truth. We take the facts that God gives us about who He is and what He promised to do, and we then live off those facts in our daily lives.

We're not cramming facts into our minds for some final exam that we'll forget the day after the test. The truth of God—the facts of God—must be lived out every day of our lives. Second Timothy 3:16–17 makes it crystal clear:

> All Scripture is breathed out by God and prof-
> itable for teaching, for reproof, for correction,
> and for training in righteousness, that the man
> of God may be competent, equipped for every
> good work.

God breathed out His Word. It's a true Word, since God cannot lie. When I'm reading the Bible, it teaches me truth. Sometimes it reproves me, because I have wandered from a certain truth. For instance, perhaps the night before, I was short with my wife, Mary. If that's the case, I guarantee you that I will be reproved in that red chair the next morning.

To be reproved is to be rebuked. In other words, the Spirit of God will make sure that a red light goes off on my spiritual dashboard. This is where correction kicks in. I then need to get up out of that red chair, set my Bible down on the desk, and go humble myself and correct the situation with Mary. I'm not just to hear the Word; I am to *do* the Word. If I am reproved, I need to make things right! That's how the Bible trains me in righteousness.

And here's another important thing to keep in mind: If I'm not listening to the Word of God in my red leather chair, and if I'm not willing to get out of that chair to go make things right with Mary, then I am disqualified to go get on a plane to speak to a group of men. I'm qualified to speak in public only if I am actively trying to apply the Word in my own home. If I'm not setting things right with Mary, then why the heck should I travel across the country to speak to men about *their* leadership? If I'm not living it out in my house, I had better stay in my house until I get things right. That's what Thomas Watson meant earlier by the statement: "The Scriptures contain in it the *credenda*, 'the things which we are to believe,' and the *agenda*, 'the things which we are to practice.'"

Why am I making such a big deal out of this? Here's why: Daniel and his friends consistently lived out their entire lives based on facts about God. When they found themselves in a tight place—which seemed to happen often—they turned to the acts and facts.

And those truths put steel into their hearts and spines.

MY TIGHT PLACE
Miami International Airport, August 19, 1966

The summer between my junior and senior years of high school, I went on a mission trip to Jamaica. But in hindsight, what I was really doing was studying in the library of the Holy Spirit—at the Jamaica branch.

August 19, 1966, started out as a great day for me. For the prior nine weeks I had been all over the country of Jamaica—a nice assignment for a sixteen-year-old.

When the opportunity came up for me to go on the trip, I had mixed feelings. I had planned on spending the summer working, and also working out, building myself up for football. Over the previous year I had diligently worked out so that I could build muscle and have a great senior season on the team. I weighed 185 pounds at Christmas, and my goal was to start the next season at 210. (It's kind of ironic that I'm *still* trying to get to 210—but from the opposite direction.) I had finally reached my goal when I left for the trip to Jamaica.

But nine weeks later I weighed 160.

Spending the majority of that time on a diet of Cheez Whiz and crackers, I pretty much quit eating. I wasn't used to the heat and humidity of Jamaica and had trouble sleeping through those hot, steamy nights under the mosquito netting. I became dehydrated and got sick at one point. But I learned some unforgettable lessons and saw the Lord do some great things. I guess you could say I had a short-term transfer from going to school in California to taking some courses in Jamaica.

The trip, however, didn't start out on good note. We had several days of training in El Paso, Texas, before we left for Jamaica. For several days, I listened to a man teach on what he called "the moral government of God." I found myself very disturbed by what he was teaching. I may have been only sixteen, but I was already picking out some stuff that just didn't pass the smell test.

The primary thing that stood out to me was that he was blatantly teaching that God didn't know the future. Somehow (according to this teacher) God had placed limits on Himself so that He didn't know what was going to happen, because it hadn't happened yet. I had never heard such a teaching in my entire life. I'd never heard it from my dad, I'd never heard it from a pastor, I'd never read it in a book, and more importantly, I had never read it in the Bible.

I was so disturbed that I made a long-distance collect call to my dad. Now back in 1966, no one ever made a long-distance collect call unless someone was on the verge of death. It cost a ton of money back then, and I'm sure when my dad heard the operator say that she had a long-distance collect call from El Paso, he must have imagined the very worst.

I told my dad what the man was teaching. And I was disturbed that all of the leaders seemed to be buying into it. If they didn't, why would they have invited him to teach? I gave my dad some details, and he told me that this could be a lesson that would serve me well for the rest of my life. Whenever I heard someone teach from the Scriptures, I had to match what they were teaching to the Bible. If it fit, everything was fine. If it didn't fit—well, it didn't fit.

That was the lesson. I remember my dad telling me that even if everyone else bought this, including the leaders, I had to make up my own mind and stand firm. I asked him if I should come home, and he suggested that I stick it out. After all, the teaching segment was over, and we were headed to Jamaica the next day. I thought that was a good idea.

Over those nine weeks, that false teaching that limited God continued to bother me. The fact is, once you start limiting God by saying He doesn't know the future, then it's an easy step to limit

Him in other ways. And that's exactly what happened as a result of the teaching in that mission organization.

What I didn't realize was that during those nine weeks in Jamaica, I would find myself in several tight places. And when I was in the middle of those pressure-packed situations, I wouldn't want to call on a "limited" God to deliver me. I would need the unlimited power of the God of the Bible to deliver me.

The nine weeks in Jamaica went by slowly. But I saw the Lord do some things that have marked my life to this day. I remember the afternoon that I was in a small village in the mountains, not far from Mandeville. I was talking with some people about a service we were planning for that evening, when suddenly someone warned me that a man was coming to kill me if I didn't stop spreading the gospel and leave immediately. The people around me were greatly alarmed. Apparently they all knew who this guy was. I wasn't sure if they were serious or not, but about five minutes later I looked across the street and saw a man staring in my direction. There was no doubt that he looked menacing, and quite frankly, demonic. Apparently he lived in the hills and would only come into town every once in a while. Everyone in the village was terrified of this guy. And I remember thinking that I needed a God who had all power—not limited power—to protect me.

I kept expecting a confrontation as the man just kept staring at me. Under my breath I was praying and asking the Lord to intervene. Suddenly that wild-looking character just turned and walked away. That was it. No confrontation and no attack. To be honest with you, it was a pretty tense situation. And then it was over. It's called acts and facts. God took care of me. He got me out of the tight place.

Another night I was in a country church way up in the mountains, and some really weird stuff started occurring in the service. Some women were praying and then they started screaming hysterically in blood-curdling fits and frenzies. The sense of demonic oppression lay thick in that room. I prayed under my breath and said, "Lord, if this isn't of You, stop this immediately." And the women who were screaming immediately—and I mean immediately—stopped. Once again, the living God came through. Acts and facts. I had believed from the Word of God that the Lord Jesus has power over the works of the devil. As a result, I simply prayed off of those facts—and He acted.

Let's return to the morning of August 19, 1966. I boarded a plane in Montego Bay that would take me to Miami. Then I needed to catch a flight out of Miami to California, so that I could get home to start football practice three days later. I had no problem getting to Miami. But when I arrived in Miami, I found myself in the middle of what became known as the great airline strike of 1966. It started on July 8 and was in its forty-first day when I landed in Miami.

I remember walking into that terminal and not believing my eyes. Hundreds and hundreds of people were literally camped out, and planes simply weren't moving. I stood in line only to be told by an agent that there was a good chance I could get a flight to New York—in five days. And from there I might have a better chance of getting to California. I was in a tight place in that moment—one of the tightest I could remember in my young life.

I talked to a man in line who had been in that terminal for five days. There was no way in the world I was going to get out of there. I had seven bucks in my pocket—and no credit cards. (Back in those days, sixteen-year-old kids didn't have credit cards, or cell phones for that matter.) It looked absolutely hopeless, and I was pretty stunned by my circumstances. How would I get home in time for football? For a young teenager, that was a very big deal.

I walked down to the far end of the terminal, stood in a corner, and turned back to look at the crowds of people who had been waiting for days and days to get out of Miami. I remember uttering a prayer—and I can still recall the exact words: "Lord, this is hopeless. I've worked my tail off for You all summer, and I need to somehow get on a plane and get out of here. Would You please get me out of here?"

About ten minutes later I saw a line forming at the National Airlines counter. I hustled over to it and got in line. The woman behind the counter told me they might have a flight leaving at midnight for Los Angeles. She took my ticket for a return to California on another airline and gave me full credit on my new ticket. As we walked to the gate, news reporters from all three networks (there used to be only three networks—imagine such hardship) covered the development. It turned out later that some friends saw me on the national news as I walked onto the plane. God got me on the first plane to move in the continental United States in forty-one days. And I made it to the first football practice. I had lost so much weight that I was worthless—but the Lord got me there.

It's called acts and facts. God made a way when there literally was no way.

That was over forty years ago, and I've seen Him do it countless times since. It's just what He does. He knows how to get you out of a tight place. He might even get union and management together and agree to end a strike so an emaciated sixteen-year-old can return home to throw up twice a day at football practice.

Now why am I bringing all of this up?

Here's why.

Life gets hard. God will lead you into some amazingly tight spaces, with no visible escape routes. And frankly, you may find yourself pretty disappointed if you were expecting your "best life now." Leonard Ravenhill said it best: "If Jesus had preached the same message that ministers preach today, He would never have been crucified."

It's going to take more than a smile to get you through. You can only stand in the evil day if you know the One who is bigger than the evil day, controls the evil day, and will bring good out of the evil day.

It all comes back to acts and facts. That's the Christian mind and the source from which Daniel drew such extraordinary courage in extraordinary times.

Looking at the way our nation seems to be heading, something tells me we're going to need a double helping of that courage.

"As God did not at first choose you because you were high, so He will not forsake you because you are low."

John Flavel

Chapter Three

FLUMMOXED AND FLABBERGASTED

One of my all-time favorite words is *flummoxed.*

And right behind it is *flabbergasted.*

You don't hear those two words used very often—they are somewhat unfamiliar to most of us. In trying to get a point across, Julius Caesar warned that you should "avoid an unfamiliar word as a ship avoids a reef."[1]

So if those two words are somewhat strange and unusual—and as a writer I'm hopefully trying to get a point across—why would I use not one but two unfamiliar words to open a chapter?

I use them because they fit … and I *like* them. What's more, as we turn to Daniel chapter 2, we see a situation develop that can only be described by two words—yep, you guessed it. *Flummoxed* and *flabbergasted.*

To be flummoxed is to be confused.

So why didn't I just go with *confused?* All I can tell you is that although they have the same meaning, *flummoxed* has a lot more sizzle than *confused.*

What about *flabbergasted?* To be flabbergasted is to be stunned or shocked. Once again, there's a lot more juice in *flabbergasted* than in *stunned* or *shocked.* So I'm sticking with *flabbergasted.*

In the opening verses of Daniel 2, we are introduced to the Babylonian king and his advisors. And you will see pretty quickly who was flummoxed and who was flabbergasted.

THE KING'S BAD NIGHT

When you're king of most of the known world and you have a bad night, *everybody* has a bad night. And when Nebuchadnezzar had a doozy of a nightmare, it became a nightmare for everyone who had the misfortune of advising him. Here's how it all came down:

> In the second year of the reign of Nebuchadnezzar, Nebuchadnezzar had dreams; his spirit was troubled, and his sleep left him. Then the king commanded that the magicians, the enchanters, the sorcerers, and the Chaldeans be summoned to tell the king his dreams. So they came in and stood before the king. And the king said to them, "I had a dream, and my spirit is troubled to know the dream." Then the Chaldeans said to the king in Aramaic, "O king, live forever! Tell your servants

the dream, and we will show the interpretation." The king answered and said to the Chaldeans, "The word from me is firm: if you do not make known to me the dream and its interpretation, you shall be torn limb from limb, and your houses shall be laid in ruins. But if you show the dream and its interpretation, you shall receive from me gifts and rewards and great honor. Therefore show me the dream and its interpretation." They answered a second time and said, "Let the king tell his servants the dream, and we will show its interpretation." The king answered and said, "I know with certainty that you are trying to gain time, because you see that the word from me is firm—if you do not make the dream known to me, there is but one sentence for you. You have agreed to speak lying and corrupt words before me till the times change. Therefore tell me the dream, and I shall know that you can show me its interpretation." The Chaldeans answered the king and said, "There is not a man on earth who can meet the king's demand, for no great and powerful king has asked such a thing of any magician or enchanter or Chaldean. The thing that the king asks is difficult, and no one can show it to the king except the gods, whose dwelling is not with flesh."

Because of this the king was angry and very furious, and commanded that all the wise men of Babylon be destroyed. So the decree went out, and the wise men were about to be killed; and they sought Daniel and his companions, to kill them. Then Daniel replied with prudence and discretion to Arioch, the captain of the king's guard, who had gone out to kill the wise men of Babylon. He declared to Arioch, the king's captain, "Why is the decree of the king so urgent?" Then Arioch made the matter known to Daniel. And Daniel went in and requested the king to appoint him a time, that he might show the interpretation to the king. (Dan. 2:1–16)

So here's what we've got.

- *Flummoxed* describes the king (vv. 1–3).
- *Flabbergasted* describes the advisors (vv. 4–15).
- *Faith* describes Daniel (v. 16).

The king had a deeply disturbing dream, and he woke up abnormally flummoxed. You've heard of acid reflux? He might have had that, too. But we know for sure that he was flummoxed. Normally he would tell his wise men the dream and they would have a staff meeting and come up with an interpretation that they would try and sell to the king.

But the king was serious this time. This dream was major-league stuff. In his anger, then, he decided that if these advisors were so smart ("How much are we paying these guys, anyway?"), they should be able tell him the interpretation *and* the dream.

The advisors were flabbergasted by such an idea. You can tell how shaken they were by the unusual tactic they took in the midst of their response. They told the king the truth! *"The thing that the king asks is difficult, and no one can show it to the king except the gods, whose dwelling is not with flesh."*

Something absolutely remarkable happens in verse 16. When Daniel found out about the crisis and that his neck was on the line along with all of the other Ivy League graduates in the king's court, he asks the king for some time. The New American Standard Bible says Daniel "requested of the king that he would give him time." But the marginal note translates it more literally: "He requested that the king would appoint a time for him." Our text above, which is the English Standard Version, translates it the same way: "Daniel went in and requested the king to appoint him a time, that he might show the interpretation to the king."

In other words, he didn't ask the king for more time; he asked the king to look at his calendar and find a time when Daniel could get thirty minutes with him (in a manner of speaking). "With remarkable faith, Daniel requested from Arioch, an appointment with the king to reveal the dream and its interpretation even before God had revealed the dream to Daniel."[2] Daniel wasn't stalling for time; he was asking the king to go ahead and set a time—and he would show up with the interpretation.

Now that's what you call faith in a tight spot.

You might also call it counterintuitive courage.

In the context of this chapter, I'd call it living off the acts and facts. I'll be honest with you, I am flummoxed and flabbergasted by Daniel's faith. Why? Because I would like to know how he got such faith at such a young age. And I am stunned and shocked by his absolute confidence that God could and would give him the

interpretation. How in the world could Daniel do that? Why wasn't
he intimidated by the king's proposed penalty for not delivering the
goods? Being "torn limb from limb" doesn't sound like my idea of a
gentle passage to the next life.

The answer is that Daniel knew the acts and the facts. He knew
who his God was and what his God could do.

Daniel was absolutely soaked and steeped in the sovereignty of
God. But he didn't get there overnight. Faith like that is built over
time. Daniel had to begin somewhere, and so do we.

MUSHROOMS ... AND OAK TREES

I want to take a time-out here and make an observation about faith.
When God implants spiritual life in our hearts by the miracle of
regeneration, we call out to Christ as our only hope of salvation. We
realize that we are lost in sin and that we have no hope of forgiveness
of sins apart from Him. Jesus told Nicodemus that he must be "born
again" (John 3:3).

When a person is born, growth becomes critical. Everyone
expects a baby to grow into adulthood, not stay in diapers. In other
words, the goal of spiritual life is the same as that of physical life:
maturity. We are to grow up in Him.

Usually the process of maturity develops slowly—as does the life
of faith. No one understood that principle better than John Newton.

Newton saw the principle in his life as he transformed from a
rebellious blasphemer who captained slave ships to a great hymn
writer and pastor. Through the years, Newton mentored many

young pastors, primarily through hundreds of letters. (Not emails, but *letters*. You remember letters, don't you?) Iain Murray explained it in detail:

> Newton regarded it as of first importance for ministers to understand that grace matures slowly. Few lessons were repeated more often to fellow ministers than this one. It comes up repeatedly:
>
> *"God works powerfully, but for the most part gently and gradually."*
>
> *"He does not teach all at once, but by degrees."*
>
> *"A Christian is not of hasty growth, like a mushroom, but rather like the oak, the progress of which is hardly perceptible, but in time becomes a great deeprooted tree."*
>
> One of his fullest treatments of this principle is in his three letters based on Christ's words on the manner in which the kingdom of God grows: "First the blade, then the ear, and after that the full corn in the ear" (Mark 4:28). On this parable Newton based on what he saw as the three stages in the life of a Christian, from its beginning to its maturity.[3]

Maturity is usually a slow process. And so is the development of faith. That's the way it works for most of us. But sometimes God breaks the mold, working swiftly in a man's life. It certainly appears that as a young man, Daniel and his three friends had extraordinary maturity and faith beyond their years. How did that come about?

The fact is, no one knows. God simply did an unusual work in their young hearts, taking a normally slow process and greatly accelerating it.

The same thing happened with Isaac Newton when he was a brilliant young student at Cambridge. It was apparent to all that he possessed extraordinary gifts and would soon become the greatest scientist of his day. But something occurred that accelerated his genius. In 1665, the black plague broke out in London, killing thousands upon thousands. It soon spread north to Cambridge, shutting down the university. Everyone fled the city, including Newton, who went to his family's remote family home in the country.

For nearly two years, Newton lived in isolation from the university and gave himself completely to his studies. He later called those years "his years of wonder.... During this time Newton accomplished more than most could accomplish in many lifetimes.... It was at Woolsthorpe that Newton left his teachers far behind, becoming the world's leading authority in mathematics and optics. He also made the first major steps in what would become his theory of gravity."[4]

Also during this time Newton invented calculus. And as he did so, he gave praise to God for his discoveries. Mitch Stokes observes that Newton believed that God revealed Himself in Scripture as well as in nature. For Newton, "to be constantly engaged in studying and probing into God's actions was true worship."[5]

"In April 1667, Cambridge was free of the plague, and Newton returned to pursue his MA. During his time away from the academy, he had become Europe's mathematician as well as its leading expert on optics, and he had laid the foundation for his revolutionary theory of gravity. Out in the country, in the mind of a twenty-four-year-old, the scientific revolution had advanced further in a few months than it had in a century."[6]

Sometimes, for purposes of His own, God accelerates growth and knowledge. He certainly did that with Isaac Newton. And Newton was a man who could quote vast sections of Scripture by memory. However, growth in faith normally comes slowly to us, just as it comes slowly to the oak tree. But growth does come. As Scripture says, "They will be called oaks of righteousness"(Isa. 61:3 NASB). Daniel and his friends were a rare breed—they were oaks at an early age.

Because of the acts and facts, Daniel didn't panic even though his life was on the line. He acted with "discretion and discernment" (Dan. 2:14 NASB) and calmly proceeded to arrange a meeting with the king to give him the interpretation.

There was just one small problem.

At that point, Daniel didn't *know* the interpretation. But Daniel knew God. And so did his friends. Together with his faithful friends, Daniel called on his faithful God.

HANDSHAKE FAITH WITH THE LIVING GOD

> Then Daniel went to his house and made the mat-
> ter known to Hananiah, Mishael, and Azariah, his
> companions, and told them to seek mercy from
> the God of heaven concerning this mystery, so that

Daniel and his companions might not be destroyed
with the rest of the wise men of Babylon. Then
the mystery was revealed to Daniel in a vision of
the night. Then Daniel blessed the God of heaven.
Daniel answered and said:

> "Blessed be the name of God forever and ever,
> to whom belong wisdom and might.
> He changes times and seasons;
> he removes kings and sets up kings;
> he gives wisdom to the wise
> and knowledge to those who have understanding;
> he reveals deep and hidden things;
> he knows what is in the darkness,
> and the light dwells with him.
> To you, O God of my fathers,
> I give thanks and praise,
> for you have given me wisdom and might,
> and have now made known to me what we asked
>   of you,
> for you have made known to us the king's matter."

Therefore Daniel went in to Arioch, whom
the king had appointed to destroy the wise men
of Babylon. He went and said thus to him: "Do
not destroy the wise men of Babylon; bring me in
before the king, and I will show the king the interpretation." (Dan. 2:17–24)

That is amazing faith—but it is based on the acts and facts.

So what is faith? And how does our faith grow? Hebrews 11:6 defines faith for us: "And without faith it is impossible to please him, for whoever would draw near to God must believe that he exists and that he rewards those who seek him."

The first ingredient in faith is believing that God exists. We have an academic system in America based on the premise that He *doesn't* exist. We are surrounded by messages from the media and from academia that God doesn't exist. But He does exist—and the evidence is overwhelming.

The second ingredient is believing that He rewards those who diligently seek Him. It's believing that God will honor His promises. It's believing that God will honor His word … and His handshake.

I don't make that last statement flippantly. When I say that faith is believing that God will honor His handshake, I say it with great reverence.

I have lived in Texas for over twenty years now. The state has some major cities—Dallas, Houston, and San Antonio—that are all among the ten largest cities in the nation. But Texas also has a lot of ranches and many, many cattle. And does the Lone Star State still have large ranches? Yes, it does. And the biggest ranch—and without a doubt the most famous—is the King Ranch. Just how big is the King Ranch? It's bigger than the state of Rhode Island. No offense, but in Texas, Rhode Island would be a county.

For years and years the cattle business was done on a promise and a handshake. That was it. Everything depended on a man's word. Two men would strike a deal over breakfast, and back in the 1860s, it would go something like this: One man would agree to round up say two thousand head out of the draws and brush of Texas and drive and deliver them to Abilene by April. The other man, who operated as a cattle broker, would agree to pay the man so many dollars per head. They would shake hands, and that was it. And the only thing that would keep either man from showing up was a deathbed. Otherwise it was a done deal.

Both men would then plan their lives on getting that deal done. And they would do so by exercising faith. The Texas driver would go find some cowboys and hire them at thirty dollars a month plus grub and put them to work finding those longhorns. He would find a cook, pay seventy-five dollars for a chuck wagon in Fort Worth, and shell out a lot more money just getting provisions together. And it was all based on faith. He lived his life believing that the other man would exist and be in Abilene by the end of April. And vice versa.

An agreement based on a handshake was actually made in *good faith*. That term is still used today. So if we will do a business deal in good faith with another individual—then why can't we do the same with the great God who cannot lie?

That's the kind of faith Daniel had in the living God. And his faith was so strong in the sovereignty and character of God that he staked his life on it. He was willing for the king to set a date—any date—and he would show up with the details of the dream and its interpretation.

His actions were all based on the fact that he believed that God existed. But the God of Israel wasn't just any pagan god—He was and is the God who made heaven and earth. Daniel could step out like this because he had soaked and steeped himself in the sovereignty of God.

That's how his faith got so strong. It started small and got increasingly bigger.

None of us starts off in the Christian life with all of the acts and facts. Most of us begin our walk down the road of faith by asking a few very important questions—and then building on that foundation. Dr. Bruce Waltke laid out the steps and progression:

> Who is God? What is his name? What is he like?
> … Israel's history is full of plots and intrigues, but
> the inspired narrators expose the human heart and
> God's responses. Their narrative plots educate the
> reader not by preaching or sermonizing, but by
> showing and enthralling.[7]

That's another way of saying that the Bible gives us acts and facts.

You might compare building our faith to building a bridge across a great chasm—like Niagara Falls.

> The Rainbow Bridge spanning Niagara Falls
> began as a kite. Those building the bridge flew
> a kite across the majestic waterway, and it came
> down on the other side of the gorge, linking
> the two sides with a thin string. Beginning with
> the string, its builders pulled more strings, then
> ropes, and eventually steel girders across the
> gorge. The more the almost unnoticeable bridge
> changed, the more it became what it was always
> meant to be.[8]

When those engineers floated a kite across Niagara Falls, a lot of people must have thought they were crazy. Zechariah 4:10 warns us not to despise "the day of small things." Some of God's greatest works begin small—and that includes our faith.

A STRING ... AND A BRIDGE

One of the things that builds our faith is seeing God answer prayer in remarkable ways. I remember how that happened to me during my freshman year in college—and it came at a very critical time. When I returned from the mission trip in Jamaica, I was pretty much burned out, and I had to be real careful right then not to get burned out on the Lord. But I was definitely fed up with a type of Christianity that was extremely man-centered and strong on rules and regulations. I didn't see a lot of God-centered truth in that mission organization (they were too busy putting limits on who God was and what He could do), and I didn't see a lot of amazing grace.

It took me about a year and a half to get my spiritual wheels back under me. As I was starting to emerge from this burnout during my freshman year of college, I began to realize that my disappointment wasn't with the Lord. Now I should hasten to say that some of the people on the Jamaican mission trip truly loved the Lord and His Word. But it's easy when you are in a discouraging and legalistic climate to see only the bad apples.

As I began to get back on my feet, I was trying to develop my spiritual disciplines: reading the Word and praying. But it didn't seem to me like I was growing much at all. What I didn't realize at the time is that this was a day of small beginnings for me. I had to fly a kite before I could build a bridge.

It was my first year in college, and I was taking some courses in broadcasting—although I later changed my major to speech communications. I was also working doing valet parking at the airport at the same time. One night I came home exhausted after chasing down cars all night long and plopped into bed. I had been trying to make sure that I spent some time in prayer each night before I hit the rack. It was a discipline I was trying to work on to make sure I didn't forget the Lord.

Well, I was in bed and just about to go unconscious when I remembered that I hadn't prayed that night. I was pretty much wasted, but I rolled out of bed, got on my knees, and said, "Lord, I've got classes at school tomorrow and there are ten thousand students up there on that hill, and at least one of them is desperate to know the truth. Would You work tomorrow and lead me to that person?"

That was it—and I rolled back into bed and went to sleep. I'm not even sure how serious I was about that prayer. But I didn't want to go to bed without praying.

I had a class at eight the next morning and made it up to the college cafeteria early enough to get a couple of doughnuts (I was sort of a health nut). I was sitting at a table by myself when a guy from one of my broadcasting classes walked over and asked if he could sit down.

"Sure," I said, "have a seat."

We had just spoken in passing a couple of times, but I remembered this guy because of his incredible voice. As a matter of fact, he is now a nationally known sports broadcaster. If I were to mention his name, you would know who he is, but back then we were just two anonymous freshmen trying to get through our first year of college. He put down his book and went to get a cup of coffee.

He came back and sat down, and I flippantly asked, "How's it going?" I expected a normal response like, "I'm fine," but I didn't get that. He just looked at me for a moment and then put his head down for about five seconds. Then he looked up at me and said, "I'm not doing real well."

I remember being a little shocked by his honesty, because I really didn't know this guy at all. I said, "I'm sorry to hear that. Is there something I could do for you?"

Then he looked me square in the eyes and said, *"I'm looking for truth, and I can't find it."*

I just about choked on my doughnut.

About seven hours before, I had mumbled something to the Lord in my slumbering stupor about leading me to one guy out of ten thousand students *who was looking for the truth.* And that's precisely what God had done. I was so flummoxed and flabbergasted that I hardly knew what to say. And then it came to me.

I said, "I've been reading a very short book by a man who was an atheist and is now a Christian. He was a professor at Oxford, and it's the clearest thing I've ever read in my life on finding truth. His name is C. S. Lewis, and the little book is called *Mere Christianity.* I just finished it. Would you be interested in taking a look at it?"

I told him a little more about the book, and he got very interested. We had about two minutes of conversation before we both had to leave for class. I happened to have the book with me at the time and gave it to him; but because it was close to the end of the semester, I don't remember ever seeing him again. I have no idea how his search for truth ended up.

All I knew was that God had answered my prayer request—to the letter. That's pretty amazing—especially when God doesn't know the future. How could God have known that guy would show up the next morning after I had prayed the prayer? What a coincidence— what a stroke of luck.

Not quite.

It was all orchestrated and planned by a sovereign God who controls everything. He knew very well that my faith needed a shot of vitamin B12. So what did He do? He flummoxed and flabbergasted me by sending the one guy out of ten thousand to my table. And it built my faith.

After the answers to prayer in Jamaica, this latest episode was another factual indicator that God could be trusted—and He wasn't limited by *anything*. And because He knew the future, He knew that my faith needed to grow. I had some things waiting for me thirty years down the road that were going to test my faith more than I would have believed. So the Lord would keep testing me and building my faith. He knew I would need much stronger faith in my forties and fifties than I had in my teens.

ANOTHER FAITH BUILDER

A number of years ago my family and I saw the Lord providentially move us into a rural property that can best be described as a small retreat center. I told the story of how this came about in my previous book, *Battle Ready*. It was truly a remarkable act of providence from the Lord. Through the generosity of the former owners, we obtained it at a significantly reduced price. So we moved in knowing that the Lord had led us to this very unique property.

And then, within a couple of months, the bottom seemed to drop out financially. Due to circumstances way beyond our control, I had five or six scheduled conferences canceled. And suddenly our cash flow began to dry up. Each month we were taking a major hit. The ministry was going in the hole, and I wasn't being paid. In fact, I quit taking a salary. We tapped out our savings and then before long we were so squeezed we started cashing out IRAs. That was something we obviously didn't want to do, and I had to pay penalties to do so. But we didn't have any other options. We didn't run a big operation—and we still don't. But after months of this financial drought, we were at Christmas and just about out of money.

During this time, the ministry was looking at somewhere around a hundred thousand dollars in bills. That's a lot of ground to make up with no conferences scheduled for the next six months. Let's just say I was having a little bit of trouble getting into the Christmas spirit.

I was trying to figure out what I had done wrong. The Lord simply wasn't blessing our work. It was Christmastime, and we would normally get a few thousand dollars in end-of-year giving. But even that wouldn't make a dent in what we needed.

I was really attempting to keep my trust in the Lord at a high level. But the week before Christmas, I just started wearing down. I was thinking in my mind that I needed to get out of this men's ministry thing and find a church somewhere that I could pastor and start generating some regular income. I was sure that the Lord had called me, and we had seen Him do some remarkable things over the years—but suddenly we were in this financial drought and there was no way out.

One day I thought, *If I went out and found $100,000 on the sidewalk, that would just get me to even.* So if out of the blue we found $100,000, we would still be in deep trouble since we had no conferences lined up for the next six months. This made absolutely no sense—so maybe I needed to get out this men's ministry deal and get a real job!

It was Thomas Watson who once said, "Where reason cannot wade, there faith may swim." My reasoning was having a hard time making it in the shallow end—and my faith was getting fatigued as I kept swimming in the deep end.

A few days before Christmas, I pulled into our driveway after meeting with some donors throughout the day. And I had absolutely nothing to show for those meetings. As I got out of the car, I had to psych myself up to be positive as I walked into the house. Truthfully I was about as down as I had ever been. But it was almost Christmas and I didn't want to depress the family, so I walked in and said hi to everyone.

We sat down for dinner, and I kept the conversation light. The kids were home from college, and I was thinking they weren't going back to college—but I wasn't going to say that right then.

I failed to mention that when I walked into the house, Mary told me that I had just missed a phone call. She told me who it was and quite frankly I was glad I missed the call. I was so discouraged I just didn't want to get on the phone at that point. The man who had called had just read one of my books and was very excited about it. I had met him at a conference, and we had renewed our acquaintance on several occasions. Mary said that he was so excited about the book that he dropped a note to me in the mail, but he also wanted to call and wish us a Merry Christmas.

As soon as I could get away with it, I excused myself and went off to bed. I wasn't tired—I was deeply depressed, absolutely worn out from the stress. I couldn't pray, and I couldn't sleep. I just needed to go to bed.

The next morning, I woke up and was depressed all over again. I was fighting it off as best as I could, but things were looking grim. I couldn't see how we could continue our ministry. Around 9:00 a.m., the phone rang, and it was one of the guys on our staff. The office was closed for Christmas, but he had gone in to tie up a few loose ends.

He told me he was checking the mail and saw a letter from the man who had called the night before.

"Oh, well, that's nice. He actually called last night before I got home," I said.

"Steve, he included a donation check to the ministry."

"Well, that was very kind of him," I replied. "I'll be sure to send a thank-you note next week."

"Steve, you need to know something. The check is for $200,000."

I absolutely could not believe my ears. I could not assimilate in my mind what I had just heard. As I held the phone next to my ear, I was in a state of shock. To be more precise, I was flummoxed and flabbergasted. I had not discussed our financial situation with that gentleman. I hadn't talked with him in months, and no one on the staff team had talked with him. He had given generously in the past, but it had been quite awhile since we had heard from him.

When I got him on the phone a couple of days later to thank him, he said, "Steve, as I read your book, it really spoke to my heart. I can't write books like you do, but I seem to do okay in business. The Lord has been real good to me. And for some reason, I just had a very strong sense that I should send a check for *that* amount."

I had been in a tight place with no visible way out. I had looked at the future and figured it was over for me. But in my weakened state of mind, I forgot the acts and facts for a couple of days. Nevertheless, the God I serve owns the cattle on a thousand hills, and He put my work and me in the mind of that fine Christian gentleman. He is now with the Lord, but I will never forget him. He was a very modest man who lived a very modest lifestyle. But he was worth millions, and he loved to give to the Lord's work. He always downplayed what he did and would simply say that God gave him favor in knowing a little bit about business.

Well, let me say this: God used that good man to flummox and flabbergast me all in the same moment. One moment my ministry was finished. The next moment it was resurrected.

I was flummoxed and flabbergasted at the goodness of God.

And my faith picked up a little more muscle for the next crisis.

That's the drill of the Christian life.

Sound familiar?

"One Almighty is more than all mighties."

William Gurnall

Chapter Four

GOLD STANDARD

Ron Wayne tries to get by each month by stretching his Social Security check and playing video poker at a casino in Nevada. He's seventy-six years old, and like a lot of people these days, he's feeling the pinch financially.

It's somewhat ironic, however, that he of all people would feel anything approaching a pinch.

After all, he is one of the founders of Apple.

When Apple was formed on April 1, 1976, Wayne signed the legal papers along with Steve Jobs and Steve Wozniak. Jobs and Wozniak each held 45 percent of the stock, and Ron Wayne had the other ten. Eleven days later he sold his shares for $800. On an impulse, he decided to get out of the infant corporation. Personal computers? Well, they probably wouldn't catch on, anyway.

So Ron Wayne took the $800 sure money and got out. But if he had held on ... his stock today would be worth $22 billion.[1] It's like the saying goes: You gotta know when to hold 'em and know when to fold 'em.

Everyone has made a financial decision that he later regretted—so no one can fault Ron Wayne. In 1976, eight hundred bucks was a nice little chunk of change. Why not take the money and run? No one wants to make a bad financial move. But in the economic chaos of these times, who's to know a wise and prudent move from a disastrous one? What's the best investment we can make as we face troubling times now and in the future?

Let me just go ahead and give you the answer to every fear, worry, and anxiety that you are having about the future. It can be summed up in just one word.

Gold.

THE GOLD STANDARD

If you're able to get together enough gold for whatever is coming, your worries are over.

Right?

That's the message that seems to come across on all of these gold commercials that show up every five minutes on cable news. As I write these words, gold is at an all-time high—over twelve hundred dollars an ounce. Gold is the ultimate trump card. If you've got enough gold, you can get through anything … or so we are told.

Ludwig Wittgenstein, the famous philosopher, had three sisters who were being held hostage by the Nazis. He got together with his brother and paid the Nazis $62 million in gold for their release.[2]

There's your proof about the power of gold. If you can just get enough of your assets in gold, you don't have to worry about what's coming down the track.

Actually that's not true.

Even in Wittgenstein's own family it wasn't true. In spite of their fabulous wealth, three of his four brothers committed suicide. His other brother, Paul, lost an arm in battle, and Ludwig himself spent time as a prisoner of war. Gold can't buy you out of every hardship.

The real gold is the sovereignty of God.

It is the sovereignty of God that will get you through anything. That's why the sovereignty of God is on every page of the book of Daniel.

When Daniel and the boys received the interpretation from the Lord, the first thing they did was to offer a prayer of thanksgiving to the living God. And as they prayed, notice how they kept emphasizing the absolute control and sovereignty of almighty God.

Daniel 2:17–23 yields three truths about the sovereignty of God. These three truths are better than any amount of gold Krugerrands, Maple Leaves, or American Eagles. God's sovereignty is the real gold you need to get through life. And remember, the sovereignty of God means that He is king and has absolute control over all things.

1. God's sovereignty magnifies His power and wisdom in my mind.

God not only has power, He also has wisdom. Power without wisdom can lead to great abuse and chaos. But our great God's power is always used in conjunction with His wisdom. Therefore,

God has power over His power. His power is always used wisely. Nor is He some impersonal Star Wars type of "force." Our God is a person. B. B. Warfield laid it on the table:

> In a word, God is pictured in the Old Testament, and that from the beginning, purely after the pattern of human personality,—as an intelligent, feeling, willing Being, like the man who is created in His image in all in which the life of a free spirit consists....
>
> Such a God could not be thought of otherwise than as the free determiner of all that comes to pass in the world which is the product of His creative act ... and the doctrine of Providence which is spread over the pages of the Old Testament fully bears out this expectation. The almighty Maker of all that is represented equally as the irresistible Ruler of all that He has made: Jehovah sits as King forever (Psalm 29:10). Even the common language of life was affected by this pervasive point of view, so that, for example, it is rare to meet such a phrase as "it rains" (Amos 4:7), and men by preference spoke of God sending rain (Psalm 65:9f, Job 36:27, Job 38:26). The vivid sense of dependence on God thus witnessed extended throughout every relation of life. Accident or chance was excluded.[3]

In other words, it didn't just rain today.

God *sent* the rain.

He has the power to do exactly that. And going back to Daniel's prayer, he praises God for His greatness, His wisdom, and His power.

Wisdom belongs to our God—all wisdom. Might and power belong to Him—nothing can stand in His way or thwart His purposes. When the seasons and the times change, it is His doing. Political leaders gain power and lose power—all at His command. He is in absolute and complete control of all things and governs every detail of life through His providential power.

As we have seen, Daniel obviously believed these truths.

Do you?

2. God's sovereignty maintains His peace in my heart and mind.

When we get a mental grip on the power of our God, it maintains His peace in our hearts—and conquers fear and worry. Notice what Daniel does after praying and honoring God for His sovereignty and power: He immediately asks to see the king.

Don't brush by that fact lightly.

This king was the most powerful ruler on the face of the earth, with the power of life and death over every one of his subjects across the world. And yet Daniel marched right into this monarch's presence, seemingly without any fear or concern for his own safety.

He could have worried that he didn't have the interpretation to the king's dream—or had it wrong. But we don't see a hint of that. His God who put the dream in the king's mind had revealed it to Daniel. His God and his God alone had the power to do such a thing. So this young man walked into the king's presence with complete confidence, because he had been in the presence of the real King—the King of Kings and the Lord of Lords.

Watch this confidence and perfect peace in Daniel's heart as he went before the king's throne:

> Therefore Daniel went in to Arioch, whom the king had appointed to destroy the wise men of Babylon. He went and said thus to him: "Do not destroy the wise men of Babylon; bring me in before the king, and I will show the king the interpretation."
>
> Then Arioch brought in Daniel before the king in haste and said thus to him: "I have found among the exiles from Judah a man who will make known to the king the interpretation." The king declared to Daniel, whose name was Belteshazzar, "Are you able to make known to me the dream that I have seen and its interpretation?" Daniel answered the king and said, "No wise men, enchanters, magicians, or astrologers can show to the king the mystery that the king has asked, but there is a God in heaven who reveals mysteries, and he has made known to King Nebuchadnezzar what will be in the latter days. Your dream and the visions of your head as you lay in bed are these: To you, O king, as you lay in bed came thoughts of what would be after this, and he who reveals mysteries made known to you what is to be. But as for me, this mystery has been

revealed to me, not because of any wisdom that I
have more than all the living, but in order that the
interpretation may be made known to the king, and
that you may know the thoughts of your mind."
(Dan. 2:24–30)

Daniel wasn't shaking in his boots because he had the peace of
the sovereign God ruling and reigning in his heart! That's what the
sovereignty of God will do for you.

It will give you True Courage.

And that's better than pure gold.

3. God's sovereignty masters the perspective of my heart and mind.

Let's get this straight. Daniel was in a foreign land because he
had lost his nation and his liberty. He was now a subject of a pagan
king, Nebuchadnezzar, who worshipped false gods. But in the midst
of all that difficulty and tragedy, this young man understood that the
sovereign God was still in control and at work. God was about to
explain to this pagan king what He was intending to do in the future.
How could that be?

Our God owns history, and He owns the future.

Is that your perspective? Or do you think that God is limited? If
you do, you don't have the God of Daniel, or the God of the Bible.

Think about it! Daniel stands there in front of the mightiest
man in the world, and he's about to convey to this powerful king
what God has determined to do concerning world powers in the

coming centuries. Daniel doesn't tell the king this *might* happen—
he tells him it *will* happen. God isn't asking for a vote on this—it's
a done deal. He's not looking for someone to second His motion. It
is His plan for the coming age, and it will stand because God rules
and reigns. As a result, Daniel's perspective on his personal history,
his present circumstances, and the future of the entire world were
based on the sovereignty of God. Warfield hammered it home for
us:

> All things without exception, indeed, are disposed
> by Him, and His will is the ultimate account of
> all that occurs. Heaven and earth and all that is in
> them are the instruments through which He works
> His ends. Nature, nations, and the fortunes of the
> individual alike present in all their changes the
> transcript of His purpose. The winds are His mes-
> sengers, the flaming fire His servant; every natural
> occurrence is His act: prosperity is His gift, and if
> calamity falls upon a man it is the Lord that has
> done it (Amos 3:5–6; Lam. 3:33–38, Isa. 47:7,
> Eccl. 7:14, Isa. 44:16).[4]

Perhaps that explains the greeting that John Newton would give
in return to people on the street. When someone would see Newton
on the street and say, "How are you today, sir?" his reply was always
the same: "I am just as God would have me."[5]

That's the sovereignty of God—and it's better than $22 billion
in Apple stock. And there's a verse in Psalms that all by itself is worth

more than $22 billion in gold: Psalm 31:15. It's very brief and con-
cise—but it can calm your soul when all hell is breaking loose around
you.

It simply says: *"My times are in Your hand"* (NKJV).

Think this through with me. Why would John Newton say, "I
am just as God would have me"? Because he knew that his times were
in God's hand. He was right where he was supposed to be, because
the all-powerful God had ordained it. He lived under the peace of
knowing that God ruled his life and his circumstances.

Daniel had the same confidence. Even though he had suffered
tremendous loss and change, he knew that his life—his times—were
under the absolute control of almighty God. He was serving as a
rookie in the Babylonian king's intern program because it was God's
plan for him. Is that what he would have chosen for his life? Probably
not. But he kept moving ahead in confidence, knowing that his steps
were ordered by the Lord. His times were under the control of a wise
and loving God. It wasn't under the control of any Babylonian king;
it was under the rule and reign of the great God who controls the
entire world.

If there was any doubt about that, the interpretation of the king's
dream put it to rest. Daniel gave a living demonstration that the
phrase "My times are in Your hand" is not only true of God's people
but for the entire world and universe as well. God owns human
history.

Daniel had the God-given ability in that moment to not only
tell the king his dream in specific detail and living color—but to also
give him the underlying meaning of that strange vision.

Let's zoom in for a minute and take a closer look.

NEBUCHADNEZZAR'S DREAM

In baseball, if you hit .300, you're a raging success. Ted Williams was the last guy to hit .400, and he is a legend … *even though he failed every six out of ten times at bat that year.*

When you stand up before a Babylonian king, however, and tell him you know exactly what he dreamed, you can't hit .300 or even .400. You'd better hit 1.000 or it's off with your head.

> You saw, O king, and behold, a great image. This image, mighty and of exceeding brightness, stood before you, and its appearance was frightening. The head of this image was of fine gold, its chest and arms of silver, its middle and thighs of bronze, its legs of iron, its feet partly of iron and partly of clay. As you looked, a stone was cut out by no human hand, and it struck the image on its feet of iron and clay, and broke them in pieces. Then the iron, the clay, the bronze, the silver, and the gold, all together were broken in pieces, and became like the chaff of the summer threshing floors; and the wind carried them away, so that not a trace of them could be found. But the stone that struck the image became a great mountain and filled the whole earth.
>
> This was the dream. (Dan. 2:31–36)

Daniel obviously hit it out of the park that day, because Nebuchadnezzar didn't say a word. And that's highly unusual for a politician. Ol' Neb had to be absolutely stunned. Speechless. The fact is, Daniel didn't even take a breath after telling him about this great image; he immediately launched into the interpretation.

Here's a thought that had to be resonating in Neb's head: If Daniel's God gave him the dream and what it showed him was absolutely accurate, then he knew the interpretation would be accurate as well. In other words, by Daniel getting the dream exactly right, he then had instant credibility with Neb as he proceeded.

> Now we will tell the king its interpretation. You, O king, the king of kings, to whom the God of heaven has given the kingdom, the power, and the might, and the glory, and into whose hand he has given, wherever they dwell, the children of man, the beasts of the field, and the birds of the heavens, making you rule over them all—you are the head of gold. Another kingdom inferior to you shall arise after you, and yet a third kingdom of bronze, which shall rule over all the earth. And there shall be a fourth kingdom, strong as iron, because iron breaks to pieces and shatters all things. And like iron that crushes, it shall break and crush all these. And as you saw the feet and toes, partly of potter's clay and partly of iron, it shall be a divided kingdom, but some of the firmness of iron shall be in it, just as you saw iron mixed with the soft clay. And as the toes of the feet were partly iron and partly clay, so the kingdom shall be partly strong and partly brittle. As you saw

the iron mixed with soft clay, so they will mix with one another in marriage, but they will not hold together, just as iron does not mix with clay. And in the days of those kings the God of heaven will set up a kingdom that shall never be destroyed, nor shall the kingdom be left to another people. It shall break in pieces all these kingdoms and bring them to an end, and it shall stand forever, just as you saw that a stone was cut from a mountain by no human hand, and that it broke in pieces the iron, the bronze, the clay, the silver, and the gold. A great God has made known to the king what shall be after this. The dream is certain, and its interpretation sure. (Dan. 2:36–45)

So what is this all about? Warren Wiersbe provides a brief summary:

The image Nebuchadnezzar beheld in his dream depicted what Jesus called "the times of the Gentiles" (Luke 21:24), a period of time that began in 605 BC when Jerusalem was taken by Nebuchadnezzar and the Babylonian army. This period will end when Christ returns to establish His kingdom (Luke 21:25–28). During the "times of the Gentiles," there will be four successive kingdoms, climaxed by a fifth kingdom that will destroy the other four and fill the earth. The fifth kingdom

is the kingdom of the Lord Jesus Christ, King of
Kings and Lord of Lords.[6]

The *ESV Study Bible* examines the four kingdoms:

> Traditional commentators through the history of
> the church have almost universally identified the
> four kingdoms as Babylon, Medo-Persia (estab-
> lished by Cyrus in 539 BC; specifically named in
> [Daniel] 8:20), Greece (under Alexander the Great,
> about 331), and Rome (the Roman Empire began
> its rule over Palestine in 63).[7]

So the head of the gold, as Daniel tells Neb, is Neb himself and
the vast Babylonian kingdom that God has placed in his hands. But
great human kingdoms don't last forever, and the Babylonians would
be taken down by Cyrus, king of the Medo-Persians in 539 BC. The
Medes and the Persians are the chest and arms of silver. By the way,
this guy Cyrus has quite a story. In Isaiah 44—45, God called Cyrus
by name and said he would be the king to return the Jews back to
Jerusalem and begin the rebuilding process. God called him by name
150 years before this occurred (Isa. 44:28).[8] The kingdom of Greece
is the belly and thighs of brass. Greece became the greatest power on
earth because of one man: Alexander the Great. And then we come
to the Roman Empire, which is described as the legs of iron and the
feet of iron and clay.

Now let's stop right here. This stuff can get pretty detailed. The
dream and interpretation of Nebuchadnezzar's dream have been

covered in great detail in numerous books and commentaries. We
could delve in the deep waters here of biblical prophecy—but we
aren't going to tackle that in these pages. As fascinating as all of that
is, constituting as it does most of the second half of the book of
Daniel, that's not my purpose here.

It's right here, however, that we need to pick up three more gold
Krugerrands.

Golden Truth 1: God owns, runs, governs, and sustains history.

I have a book next to me as I write—a book on the doctrine
of God. The author is John Feinberg, it is over eight hundred
pages long, and its title says it all: *No One Like Him.* In his preface,
Feinberg briefly describes the motivation that led him to write the
thick volume:

> I must have been crazy to think that I could write
> a book on the doctrine of God. Still, like the moth
> drawn to a flame, I keep coming back to this topic.
> In one way or another, it has been the concern of
> much of my adult intellectual thought and publica-
> tions. Of course, the subject is more than worthy of
> our attention, *because nothing could be more impor-*
> *tant than coming to understand God better* and hence
> worship him more.[9]

Nothing could be more important! That's it. Nothing could be
more than knowing the acts and facts. That's why John Feinberg

has spent his adult life studying the doctrine of God. That is the key to surviving when things are falling apart all around you. Your reaction to the days of increasing difficulty will be determined by how well you know God and who He is. In fact, that's what eternal life is.

Eternal life isn't just "living forever"—it's getting to know God more and more. Note the words of the Lord Jesus in John 17:3: *"And this is eternal life, that they know you the only true God, and Jesus Christ whom you have sent."*

To know God is not only to learn more about who He is but also to live in moment-to-moment relationship with Him as your Father.

It's a great reminder that God owns, runs, governs, and sustains history—and each of our lives as well.

Golden Truth 2: God has built decay and decline into great nations.

You've heard of the rise and fall of great nations. That's the story of history, and it definitely applies to the kingdoms represented in Nebuchadnezzar's dream. Wiersbe again makes the point:

> The dream reveals that human enterprises decline as time goes on. The massive and awesome image not only changed in value from head to foot— from gold to clay—but it also changed in strength, finally ending in feet made of iron mixed with clay.

Actually, the statue was top-heavy, for the atomic weight of gold is ten times that of clay. From age to age, nations and kingdoms appear strong and durable, but they're always in danger of falling over and crashing.[10]

Golden Truth 3: Christ is coming back with a kingdom that will never be destroyed.

After Daniel tells Nebuchadnezzar of the fourth kingdom, which we know to be the Roman Empire, we read these words in Daniel 2:44–45:

> And in the days of those kings the God of heaven will set up a kingdom that shall never be destroyed, nor shall the kingdom be left to another people. It shall break in pieces all these kingdoms and bring them to an end, and it shall stand forever, just as you saw that a stone was cut from a mountain by no human hand, and that it broke in pieces the iron, the bronze, the clay, the silver, and the gold. A great God has made known to the king what shall be after this. The dream is certain, and its interpretation sure.

We live in a lawless time—a time where every man and woman does what is right in their own eyes. Should this surprise us? Of

course not. Because we know very well that God is setting up the
world for the Antichrist. One of the terms that is applied to the
Antichrist is "man of lawlessness." So the table of lawlessness is in
the process of being set. But one day the Lord Jesus will come back
and destroy lawlessness and set up His kingdom of righteousness.
I appreciate the worldview of the wise old Bible teacher J. Vernon
McGee:

> God's form of government is going to be one of
> the most strict forms of government that the world
> has ever seen. I do not think a rooster is going to
> crow in that day without His permission to do so.
> The Lord Jesus Christ is going to be a dictator, and
> if you are not willing to bow to Him, I don't think
> you would even want to be in His kingdom when
> He establishes it upon the earth. Maybe it is good
> that He has another place for folk like that, because
> it will not be pleasant for them to be here—they
> wouldn't enjoy it at all. God's form of government
> is the absolute rule of a king, the sovereignty of one
> ruler. It is going to be autocratic, dictatorial, and
> His will is going to prevail. That is the reason it is
> well for you and me to practice bowing to Him and
> acknowledging Him. He is going to take over one
> of these days.[11]

I don't know about you, but for me that day can't get here soon
enough.

NEBUCHADNEZZAR'S RESPONSE

> Then King Nebuchadnezzar fell upon his face and
> paid homage to Daniel, and commanded that an
> offering and incense be offered up to him. The king
> answered and said to Daniel, "Truly, your God
> is God of gods and Lord of kings, and a revealer
> of mysteries, for you have been able to reveal this
> mystery." Then the king gave Daniel high honors
> and many great gifts, and made him ruler over the
> whole province of Babylon and chief prefect over
> all the wise men of Babylon. Daniel made a request
> of the king, and he appointed Shadrach, Meshach,
> and Abednego over the affairs of the province of
> Babylon. But Daniel remained at the king's court.
> (Dan. 2:46–49)

It all rang true, and Nebuchadnezzar knew it.

The king had no doubt that this was the real deal, and it shook
him to the core. Suddenly it was Nebuchadnezzar himself who was
declaring the acts and facts: "Truly, your God is God of gods and
Lord of kings, and a revealer of mysteries, for you have been able to
reveal this mystery."

And in response, he promoted Daniel to the post of prime
minister of Babylon. Daniel started Daniel 2 as a rookie intern, and
he finished in Daniel 2 as prime minister. And in between those
two bookends, his life was threatened by a king who could match
violence and blood with any tyrant. But the sovereign God made a

way for Daniel and his friends. Just as He made a way for Joseph and promoted him when all hope was lost, so He made a way for Daniel. This is the glory of God's sovereignty and providence. And it is designed to calm and quiet our hearts as we face an uncertain future in our troubled nation. We cannot forget that God is in charge and that His providence works in every detail of our lives.

History is connected. Every nation has its place, and every person has his or her place. Nothing is random or by chance. God has a purpose in the midst of all the events of life, including the disappointments and setbacks. And amazingly, they are all tied together.

Daniel lost his liberty and lived under tyranny. But even under tyranny God was at work. God caused that proud, unbelieving king to have a dream, and He used Daniel to unlock His plan for the ages to that same king. None of these events were random or accidental. Even though certain pieces of Daniel's life made no sense at certain times, a divine thread ran through the story of his life.

The sovereign God is in control of the details of your life and of history. Nothing can thwart His plan for the nations or for you, your children, and your grandchildren. Those are the acts and facts. Those truths about His sovereignty steady us and steel us in trying times. They are worth many times beyond their weight in gold.

John MacArthur once gave a message where he stated that wherever he is in the world, he sleeps well. And the reason he sleeps well is because of his theology.[12]

How well are you sleeping in the midst of your difficulties and challenges? It all depends on your theology. It all depends on what you believe about God's sovereignty and providence. How well you sleep tonight is directly related to what you believe about God and

His control over all of history and the entire world. It's all linked together.

What was the title of John Feinberg's book?

No One Like Him.

That pretty much sums it up. The more you get to know and understand Him, the more you realize that there is no one like Him. He is your hope and He is your gold.

Take courage from that.

*"The being of God may as well fail
as the promise of God."*

Timothy Cruso

Chapter Five

LOCK, STOCK, AND BARREL

In 1790, watchmaker and gunsmith Honoré Le Blanc made an astonishing demonstration in France before a thousand politicians and military leaders. What he demonstrated would make the jaws of the onlookers drop in utter astonishment.

Le Blanc had come up with the invention of interchangeable parts—and he proved the concept by assembling a musket in front of his distinguished audience. In 1790, this concept absolutely rocked not only his audience but also the entire world.

Le Blanc had made a thousand muskets and put all of their parts in separate bins.[1] "[He] had worked out a system for making gun parts to a standardized pattern, so if a part broke, it could be replaced immediately by another part that would fit the gun exactly."[2] His muskets were comprised of three parts. One could randomly grab a part from each of the bins and construct a musket. Thomas Jefferson, who had been given an earlier demonstration by Le Blanc, wrote a report to the American government: "I put several together myself, taking pieces at hazard as they came to hand, and they fitted in the most perfect manner."[3]

Kenneth Hopper describes the sheer genius of the concept:

> The lock, which is so-called because of a supposed resemblance to a door lock, is the firing mechanism in a musket, the two other parts being the wooden stock or butt and the metal barrel. Since the lock, the stock and the barrel constituted the entire gun, it is easy to see how, taken together, the words came to mean "completely."[4]

So the origin of the term *lock, stock, and barrel* came from Le Blanc's startling invention of interchangeable parts. Before Le Blanc's invention, it would sometimes take days for a gunsmith to construct a musket. But now with interchangeable parts, a finished and complete musket could be assembled in mere minutes. It was nothing short of revolutionary.

My contention is that there is an interchangeable part that fits immediately into the life of any and every true believer in Jesus Christ—old or young, ancient saint or brand-new Christian. It fit in the life of the apostle Paul, and it fits perfectly well—hand in glove—in your life as well, if you have placed your faith in Christ.

You can easily identify this key component in the life of Daniel, and in this chapter, we'll see up close what an integral part it played in the lives of Shadrach, Meshach, and Abednego.

What is that key component and central question?

It's simply this: *Will you, or will you not, trust God for your future?*

A QUESTION FOR ALL OF US

That's always the question, isn't it? In some way, shape, or form you are facing that question in your life today—will you trust God for your future? Or maybe you're having to trust God more specifically for someone else. It's *their* future that seems up for grabs, with everything going against them. You love and care for them, but it's out of your control. So even though it's their future, because you love them and are on their team, you, too, are having to trust God to come through for them.

Trusting God for your future is a major piece of the Christian life. In that sense, it's interchangeable. It's in your life and mine. Everyone who follows the Lord from the heart is learning to trust God with his or her future.

THE MISSING SABBATH YEARS

Here's a less intense question for you: Why were Daniel, Shadrach, Meshach, and Abednego in Babylon in the first place? Why weren't they back home in Jerusalem? A major part of the answer to that question is that their forefathers refused to trust God with their future. Specifically I'm referring to the Sabbath years that God commanded Israel to obey. You are familiar that Israel was to observe the

Sabbath and take one day out of seven as a day of rest. It's right there in the Ten Commandments:

> Remember the Sabbath day, to keep it holy. Six days you shall labor, and do all your work, but the seventh day is a Sabbath to the LORD your God. On it you shall not do any work, you, or your son, or your daughter, your male servant, or your female servant, or your livestock, or the sojourner who is within your gates. For in six days the LORD made heaven and earth, the sea, and all that is in them, and rested on the seventh day. Therefore the LORD blessed the Sabbath day and made it holy. (Ex. 20:8–11)

But there was also a Sabbath *year,* and here's where it gets very interesting. Leviticus 25:3–5 clearly paints the picture:

> For six years you shall sow your field, and for six years you shall prune your vineyard and gather in its fruits, but in the seventh year there shall be a Sabbath of solemn rest for the land, a Sabbath to the LORD. You shall not sow your field or prune your vineyard. You shall not reap what grows of itself in your harvest, or gather the grapes of your undressed vine. It shall be a year of solemn rest for the land.

When the people of Israel heard this, it had to scare them to death. Why would it frighten them? Because if they weren't allowed to plant crops in the seventh year, it would force them to trust God for their futures. Trusting God for your future is an interchangeable part that can be found way back in the earliest years of the Old Testament. Right on the heels of commanding them to let the land rest in the seventh year, God made them a promise in Leviticus 25:20–22 to take away their fears:

> And if you say, "What shall we eat in the seventh year, if we may not sow or gather in our crop?" I will command my blessing on you in the sixth year, so that it will produce a crop sufficient for three years. When you sow in the eighth year, you will be eating some of the old crop; you shall eat the old until the ninth year, when its crop arrives.

God promised to provide enough for them in the sixth year of harvest to get them through the next three years. So the question would be, would they trust God to fulfill His promise? Could they trust Him to provide for their futures? That was the central issue at work here.

Back in 1858, P. B. Power diagnosed the problem:

> The dear children of the Lord are continually detecting themselves in unbelief. At one moment they are leaning upon human instrumentality, at another they are at their wit's end; now they are full of terror at an immediate prospect of danger, and now they lose all rest in God; all which evils

proceed from the want of simple faith, of child-like trust. *God loves trust; it honors Him; he who trusts the most shall sorrow least. If there were continual trust there would be continual peace.* [italics mine][5]

In Leviticus 26:33–35, the Lord tells them what He will do if they refused to obey His command and observe the year of Sabbath rest:

> And I will scatter you among the nations, and I will unsheathe the sword after you, and your land shall be a desolation, and your cities shall be a waste.
>
> Then the land shall enjoy its Sabbaths as long as it lies desolate, while you are in your enemies' land; then the land shall rest, and enjoy its Sabbaths. As long as it lies desolate it shall have rest, the rest that it did not have on your Sabbaths when you were dwelling in it.

So back to our original question: Why did Daniel and his three friends find themselves in the foreign land of Babylon? Charles Dyer and Eugene Merrill sum it up:

> Why did God predict that the Babylonian Exile would last seventy years? Because this was the number of times the people had failed to observe God's law of a "Sabbath rest" for the land. God had decreed that every seventh year the land was to lie

fallow (Leviticus 25:3–5). If the people failed to follow this command, God would remove them from
the land to enforce this "Sabbath rest" (Leviticus
26:33–35). The writer of 2 Chronicles indicated
that the seventy-year Babylonian captivity allowed
the land to enjoy its "Sabbath rests" (2 Chronicles
36:20–21).[6]

Here's how that passage from 2 Chronicles reads:

> He took into exile in Babylon those who had
> escaped from the sword, and they became servants
> to him and to his sons until the establishment of
> the kingdom of Persia, to fulfill the word of the
> LORD by the mouth of Jeremiah, until the land had
> enjoyed its Sabbaths. All the days that it lay desolate
> it kept Sabbath, to fulfill seventy years.

So one of the main reasons for the nation of Judah being invaded
and swept away into captivity was their outright refusal to trust God
for the Sabbath years. God told them not to farm in the seventh
year, to let the land rest. He promised to give them in the sixth year
a harvest so abundant that it would last for three years.

But did they trust Him with their futures?

Did they obey and believe that God could be trusted with their
needs?

No, they didn't. *Not once* did they obey God and rest the land in
the seventh years. Not even under godly kings like David, Solomon,

Hezekiah, and Josiah. This neglect had gone on for 490 years. How do we know that? Because God said they owed him seventy years for seventy years of missed sabbatical years. They were in Babylon because they had refused to trust God with their futures. And that's why Daniel, Shadrach, Meshach, and Abednego were in Babylon instead of Jerusalem.

In other words, they were there because of the sins of their forefathers. But now they themselves were about to be tested to see if they would trust God for *their* futures. This well-known story in Daniel 3 breaks down into four parts:

1. The Federal Regulation (3:1–7)
2. The Principled Refusal (3:8–18)
3. The Supernatural Rescue (3:19–27)
4. The Regulation Reversed (3:28–30)

THE FEDERAL REGULATION

King Nebuchadnezzar made an image of gold, whose height was sixty cubits and its breadth six cubits. He set it up on the plain of Dura, in the province of Babylon. Then King Nebuchadnezzar sent to gather the satraps, the prefects, and the governors, the counselors, the treasurers, the justices, the magistrates, and all the officials of the provinces to come to the dedication of the image that King Nebuchadnezzar had set up. Then the satraps, the prefects, and the governors, the counselors, the treasurers, the justices, the magistrates, and all the officials of the provinces gathered for the dedication of the image that King Nebuchadnezzar had set up. And they stood before the image that Nebuchadnezzar had set up. And the herald proclaimed aloud, "You are commanded, O peoples, nations, and languages, that when you hear the sound of the horn, pipe, lyre, trigon, harp, bagpipe, and every kind of music, you are to fall down and worship the golden image that King Nebuchadnezzar has set up. And whoever does not fall down and worship shall immediately be cast into a burning fiery furnace." Therefore, as soon as all the peoples heard the sound of the horn, pipe, lyre, trigon, harp, bagpipe, and every kind of music, all the peoples, nations, and languages fell down and worshiped the golden image that King Nebuchadnezzar had set up. (Dan. 3:1–7)

Way outside of Babylon on the plains, Nebuchadnezzar had built a massive statue. Undoubtedly he built it out on the plains to accommodate the tens of thousands who would come from all over the Babylonian Empire to obey his order. This statue was ninety feet high, nine feet in width, and was made out of solid gold. Many Bible scholars believe that the purpose of this regulation to worship the statue was given in order to drive home that every far-reaching nation and state was under Nebuchadnezzar's authority. It was his way of sealing in everyone's mind that he was the absolute ruler. And if anyone doubted that he was in charge of the greatest empire on earth, they would quickly be shown their way into the ovens.

That's the way it was when Hitler came to power in Germany. In 1933, the German philosopher Martin Heidegger said, "The Führer, and he alone, is the present and future law of Germany."[7] In those tyrannical days in Germany, one man was the law. And to disagree with him, like Nebuchadnezzar, was to buy a ticket to the ovens.

Gathering a great crowd to bow down before the state is nothing new. The first time it was tried came with the Tower of Babel in Genesis 11. And as the *ESV Study Bible* point outs, the Tower of Babel is tied to Nebuchadnezzar's statue hundreds of years later in Babylon:

> This episode is significantly more important than its length suggests. It presents a unified humanity using all its resources to establish a city that is the antithesis of what God intended when he created the world. The tower is a symbol of human autonomy, and the city builders see themselves as determining and establishing their own destiny without any reference to the Lord. This verse links the name of the city, **Babel** (Hb. *babel*), with the verb *balal*, which means "to confuse, to mix, to mingle." ... But *babel* is also the name used in the Old Testament for the city of Babylon. As a city, Babylon symbolizes humanity's ambition to dethrone God and make the earth its own (see Revelation 17–18).[8]

Nebuchadnezzar's statue was an attempt to demonstrate that he was independent from any god—he was the ultimate ruler. This is always the motivation of tyranny, whatever form it may take.

Saddam Hussein was not ignorant of Nebuchadnezzar's greatness and his empire. In fact, it is pretty clear that everything that Saddam did was to restore the rule and reign of Nebuchadnezzar. Dr. Charles Dyer spent time in Iraq doing research on the link between the two crazed rulers:

> Imagine, if you will, a ruler determined to stamp his name on the pages of history. His goal is complete domination of all surrounding nations, and he has built an extensive army capable of carrying out his wishes. He holds absolute power, and he does not hesitate to execute those who pose even a remote threat to his leadership. People have been arrested and imprisoned for the simple crime of not revering his image.
>
> Yet his military might is not his only claim to fame. He also sees himself as a patron of culture; of poets, artists, and architects. Even the bricks in Babylon bear his name as the personal overseer of its completion.
>
> Is this a fair description of Saddam Hussein? Yes, but it also accurately describes Nebuchadnezzar II, the Babylonian king whose empire once stretched from sea to sea. In his day, the lands of what are now Iraq, Saudi Arabia, Syria, Lebanon, Jordan, Israel,

and Kuwait were all under Babylonian control. In
August 1990, Saddam Hussein reclaimed a portion
of that early empire and invaded Kuwait. Could
he possibly hope to reclaim the entire kingdom of
Nebuchadnezzar?[9]

As we know, Saddam came up a little bit short in his attempt to
emulate the great and ruthless Nebuchadnezzar. Saddam didn't come
up short in his ruthlessness, maiming, poisoning, and raping, but he
sure came up short of rebuilding the empire. But it's important to
know that Nebuchadnezzar and Saddam were very similar in their
willingness to torture and murder in order to intimidate their people
to submit. That's what this statue was meant to do. It was a way of
intimidating the people of the far-reaching empires to bow out of
fear to the statue. It was a federal regulation—and we know all about
those, don't we?

Something very similar to this happened in the nation of Ghana
in the 1960s. Kwame Nkrumah, a man who had a master's degree
in theology, had risen through the political ranks, named himself
president, and made Ghana a one-party state. He rode to his ironlike
socialistic rule on the power of his personality and encouraged his
followers to call him *Osagyefo,* "the Redeemer."[10] He ordered that a
slightly larger-than-life statue of himself be built and placed in front
of the Ghana Parliament. His motto was on the side of the statue:
"Seek ye first the political kingdom and all other things shall be
added unto you." The statue was torn down after a coup in 1966.[11]

Tyranny is nothing new. First John 2:18 states: "Children, it is
the last hour, and as you have heard that antichrist is coming, so now

many antichrists have come." There will be a coming antichrist, but there have always been little antichrists. Tyrants, in whatever country they are found or in whatever age, are dedicated to establishing their agenda and their rule. And they demand submission and obedience to their programs and agenda. This is demonic tyranny, and it is coming our way. We can learn from Shadrach, Meshach, and Abednego about how to prepare ourselves.

THE PRINCIPLED REFUSAL

Therefore at that time certain Chaldeans came forward and maliciously accused the Jews. They declared to King Nebuchadnezzar, "O king, live forever! You, O king, have made a decree, that every man who hears the sound of the horn, pipe, lyre, trigon, harp, bagpipe, and every kind of music, shall fall down and worship the golden image. And whoever does not fall down and worship shall be cast into a burning fiery furnace. There are certain Jews whom you have appointed over the affairs of the province of Babylon: Shadrach, Meshach, and Abednego. These men, O king, pay no attention to you; they do not serve your gods or worship the golden image that you have set up."

Then Nebuchadnezzar in furious rage commanded that Shadrach, Meshach, and Abednego be brought. So they brought these men before the king. Nebuchadnezzar answered and said to them, "Is it true, O Shadrach, Meshach, and Abednego, that you do not serve my gods or worship the golden image that I have set up? Now if you are ready when you hear the sound of the horn, pipe, lyre, trigon, harp, bagpipe, and every kind of music, to fall down and worship the image that I have made, well and good. But if you do not worship, you shall immediately be cast into a burning fiery furnace. And who is the god who will deliver you out of my hands?"

Shadrach, Meshach, and Abednego answered and said to the king, "O Nebuchadnezzar, we have no need to answer you in this matter. If this be so, our God whom we serve is able to deliver us from the burning fiery furnace, and he will deliver us out of your hand, O king. But if not, be it known to you, O king, that we will not serve your gods or worship the golden image that you have set up." (Dan. 3:8–18)

What the king was asking them to do was to violate the first two commandments. He wanted nothing less than their total allegiance to him and to the state. But that was something that God had forbidden:

You shall have no other gods before me.

> You shall not make for yourself a carved image, or any likeness of anything that is in heaven above, or that is in the earth beneath, or that is in the water under the earth. You shall not bow down to them or serve them, for I the LORD your God am a jealous God, visiting the iniquity of the fathers on the children to the third and the fourth generation of those who hate me, but showing steadfast love to thousands of those who love me and keep my commandments. (Ex. 20:3–6)

Nebuchadnezzar imagined that he had those three godly young men backed into a corner with his authority and power. He held the power of life and death over them ... or at least he did in his mind. But that's not how Shadrach, Meshach, and Abednego saw it. In his fury, the king wanted to force their hands in regard to their immediate future. They could continue to live their lives in Babylon with all of the comforts and privileges granted to them when they were promoted (Dan. 2:49), or they could experience an immediate end to their earthly existence.

I remember hearing Francis Schaeffer speak in Oakland, California, in 1979. In response to a question about the future of America, he said something to the effect that he believed that America would one day wind up as a dictatorship. He could foresee a situation where, due to some kind of great crisis or series of crises, Americans would give up their freedoms if they could be promised two things: personal peace and affluence.

Now that's exactly what was put before Shadrach, Meshach, and Abednego. Let me remind you that they had already lost their freedoms because Nebuchadnezzar had conquered their nation. But because of the goodness of God, they had been given a remarkable promotion and place of status and influence. And now they were facing a dilemma that required an immediate answer. They could opt for continued personal peace and affluence. All they had to do was to make a quick bow.

But these men had actually settled this issue long before the current crisis overtook them.

They would obey the Lord.

It wasn't even up for discussion.

Compromise was never an option.

They didn't need to give the king an answer on his option of bowing to the image, because it was never really an option at all. Their minds were steadfast. They would stand firm and stand tall. "They had determined and resolved in their inmost souls, not to depart a single inch from the true and lawful worship of God."[12] I love that phrase from John Calvin's commentary: *"Not to depart a single inch."*

It all came down to trusting God for their futures. They knew that their God had the power to deliver them. But even if He didn't—even if their bodies were vaporized in those flames—it wasn't going to change their minds. Idolatry was not an option, no matter what the consequence might be. They would trust the Lord God with their futures. If He delivered them with His great power, so be it. And if He didn't, so be it. Their future was in His hands.

When the early Christian Cyprian was given an opportunity to deny Christ and save his life, he replied, "There can be no deliberation in a matter so sacred."[13] That was the response not only of Cyprian but also of Shadrach, Meshach, and Abednego.

SUPERNATURAL RESCUE

Then Nebuchadnezzar was filled with fury, and the expression of his face was changed against Shadrach, Meshach, and Abednego. He ordered the furnace heated seven times more than it was usually heated. And he ordered some of the mighty men of his army to bind Shadrach, Meshach, and Abednego, and to cast them into the burning fiery furnace. Then these men were bound in their cloaks, their tunics, their hats, and their other garments, and they were thrown into the burning fiery furnace. Because the king's order was urgent and the furnace overheated, the flame of the fire killed those men who took up Shadrach, Meshach, and Abednego. And these three men, Shadrach, Meshach, and Abednego, fell bound into the burning fiery furnace.

Then King Nebuchadnezzar was astonished and rose up in haste. He declared to his counselors, "Did we not cast three men bound into the fire?" They answered and said to the king, "True, O king." He answered and said, "But I see four men unbound, walking in the midst of the fire, and they are not hurt; and the appearance of the fourth is like a son of the gods."

Then Nebuchadnezzar came near to the door of the burning fiery furnace; he declared, "Shadrach, Meshach, and Abednego, servants of the Most High God, come out, and come here!" Then Shadrach, Meshach, and Abednego came out from the fire. And the satraps, the prefects, the governors, and the king's counselors gathered together and saw that the fire had not had any power over the bodies of those men. The hair of their heads was not singed, their cloaks were not harmed, and no smell of fire had come upon them. (Dan. 3:19–27)

There are many critical points to observe out of this event. But the main point is that these young men were rescued by an appearance of the Lord Jesus Christ. You might be thinking that's a problem, because the Lord Jesus hadn't come to earth yet, and you would be correct. But this is what is known as a theophany (God appearing visibly) or more accurately, a *Christophany* (Christ appearing visibly before His virgin birth). Robert Duncan Culver observes that the Lord Jesus appeared in the Old Testament "to Hagar (Genesis 16), to Abram (Genesis 18), to Jacob (Genesis 32), and others and is called Jehovah (the Sacred Name; 'LORD' is used in most translations) in Genesis 18:18–21 and God in Exodus 3:2. 'Wonderful' is a 'name' for the predicted Christ in Isaiah 9:6 and 'wonderful' is also the name of 'the angel of the Lord' in the annunciation of the birth of Samson to his parents (Judges 13:18)."[14]

It was this wonderful Savior whom Nebuchadnezzar saw in the furnace with Shadrach, Meshach, and Abednego.

Now here's a question: Why was the Lord Jesus in the fire with them? He was there with them to rescue them, because He was in charge of their futures. We have said throughout this chapter that the essence of the story is the question, *would they trust God for their futures?* And here was the Son of God Himself, the Lord Jesus Christ, showing up to rescue them and preserve them.

I like the way the old King James Version recorded Neb's words: "Lo, I see four men loose, walking in the midst of the fire, and they have no hurt; and the form of the fourth is like the Son of God" (Dan. 3:25).

Why did the Lord Jesus show up?

Because He wasn't done with them yet.

He still had a work for them to do. They weren't finished yet. So He showed up to rescue them. He had created them in the womb and planned all of their days, and this furnace wasn't to be the end. He had more in mind for them to do. In Psalm 139:16, David declared: "Your eyes saw my unformed substance; in your book were written, every one of them, the days that were formed for me, when as yet there was none of them."

God knew these men when He formed them in the womb. To Jeremiah the prophet He said, "Before I formed you in the womb I knew you, and before you were born I consecrated you; I appointed you a prophet to the nations" (Jer. 1:5). God knew Jeremiah before He formed him and called him to be a prophet. God had a work for

Jeremiah to do. He had a work for Daniel and his three friends to do. And that work was set before the foundations of the earth. All of their days were written in His book before the days existed.

What does that mean to you and me?

It means that the Lord Jesus in eternity past determined the moment of our conception, the moment of our birth, and the moment of our death (Heb. 9:27).

And the three Hebrew teenagers were rescued because God had planned and provided for their future. He had determined the number of their days, and their days weren't up yet. So He rescued them and saved them.

All of this applies to you, and I would ask you to zero in on this thought: *You can't die until your work is done.* They may talk about you behind your back and they might even rough you up—but they can't kill you until your work is done. That's why God Himself stepped into that furnace and rescued them.

You might be thinking that God doesn't work like that anymore, but you couldn't be further from the truth. He works all of the time in our lives to save us and rescue us. Was there ever an incident in your life where you should have been killed—and you obviously weren't? That was His hand at work in your life, as clearly as He was at work in that Babylonian furnace. Psalm 68:19–20 declares:

> Blessed be the Lord, who daily bears our burden,
>   The God who is our salvation.
> God is to us a God of deliverances;
>   And to GOD the Lord belong escapes from death.
>   (NASB)

The fact of the matter is you can trust Him with your future—long term and short term. He's got every day of your future covered. He *daily* bears our burden. He *daily* delivers us. That's why you don't have to be paralyzed by what may happen tomorrow. He's got tomorrow covered. You've heard of living paycheck to paycheck? (Maybe you've heard of it because you're doing it.) In the Scriptures, we are told to live day by day. It doesn't mean that we don't invest or save, but if a crisis hits and you lose your job and go through all of your savings, He will be there each day to deliver you.

Oh, and by the way, how did you get that savings in the first place? He gave it to you. Deuteronomy 8:18 says that "it is He who [gives] you power to make wealth" (NASB). Whatever you have is from His hand. And when you run out of what you have, He'll make sure a delivery shows up to get you through that day.

George Müller and his two thousand orphans knew all about that. For over sixty years, they saw God provide daily for them in Bristol, England. Müller started his work for orphans on December 9, 1835. He kept a meticulous daily diary in which he kept track of the funds received and the expenses. What was so unique about Müller is that he truly and literally believed that he could trust God for his future and the futures of the orphans. Eventually he had over two thousand children in his care and the responsibility of feeding, clothing, and educating them.

In the sixty years of his ministry, Müller never once asked anyone to make a contribution. He didn't send out letters making financial appeals. He believed that he could trust God for the future and for the daily needs of the children. In his diary account of January 4, 1853, when he had three hundred children in the orphanage, he penned these words:

> Those people are entirely mistaken who suppose that
> the work is now no longer a work of faith, as it used
> to be in former years. It is true, we have now a larger
> income than we used to have in the years 1838,
> 1839, and 1840: but it is also true that our expenses
> are three times as great. We have no regular income
> now; even as we had none then. We ask no human
> being for help; even as we did not then. We depend
> alone upon God, by His grace; even as we did then.[15]

When you read through Müller's massive diary, it's a constant testimony of a man who saw God deliver him day by day. There were times in the morning when they were out of food—but those kids never missed a breakfast, lunch, or dinner. God showed up daily.

Now think this through for a minute. If God has a work for you to do, and you can't die until you complete that work (Eph. 2:10), then isn't it His job to keep you alive each day so that you can finish that task? That means giving you work so that you can provide for your family: buy groceries, pay the mortgage and tuition. To the Lord belongs escapes from death—physical deaths and financial deaths. He always makes a way. And even Nebuchadnezzar had to admit that.

THE REGULATION REVERSED

> Nebuchadnezzar answered and said, "Blessed be
> the God of Shadrach, Meshach, and Abednego,

who has sent his angel and delivered his servants,
who trusted in him, and set aside the king's command, and yielded up their bodies rather than
serve and worship any god except their own God.
Therefore I make a decree: Any people, nation, or
language that speaks anything against the God of
Shadrach, Meshach, and Abednego shall be torn
limb from limb, and their houses laid in ruins, for
there is no other god who is able to rescue in this
way." Then the king promoted Shadrach, Meshach,
and Abednego in the province of Babylon. (Dan.
3:28–30)

Nebuchadnezzar said it himself: "There is no other god who is
able to rescue in this way." To the Lord belongs escapes from death,
and Neb could not deny it.

But what if those three teenagers hadn't been delivered? What
if they had instantly perished in the flames of Nebuchadnezzar's
furnace?

It's a simple fact, of course, that not everyone who stands for his
or her faith in Christ is delivered. Thousands upon thousands, even
tens of thousands, have died for their unwillingness to deny Christ.
How do we respond when God doesn't deliver?

I think we must look at these instances again through the lens
of Scripture. When a believer dies for his or her faith, we must realize that the time of that death was part of God's eternal plan (Ps.
139:16). Job 14:1, 5 declares the same truth: "Man, who is born
of woman, is short-lived and full of turmoil.... Since his days are

determined, the number of his months is with You; and his limits You have set so that he cannot pass" (NASB).

We cannot live a minute beyond our appointed time. And God ordains it all. Why do some die in infancy and others live a full, long life? We don't know. Certainly God knows, but He has chosen not to reveal His reasons to us. Deuteronomy 29:29 says that "the secret things belong to the LORD our God, but the things revealed belong to us and our sons forever" (NASB). Some things God has revealed and others He has kept secret. The death of a child, of a spouse, of a foreign missionary, or of a teenager in the prime of life—we shake our heads and wonder why. And we get no response. To us the reasons remain a secret. But the answer will come to us one day in the future from our God who is good and does good (Ps. 119:68).

Until that time, we must wait and trust Him for our futures.

And if in the meantime we lack courage, we wait on Him for that as well.

"As death is the last enemy, so pride is the last sin that shall be destroyed in us."

John Boys

Chapter Six

THE HARD WAY

When Peter Hitchens was fifteen years of age and attending boarding school at Cambridge, he lit a match and set fire to his Bible. It had been a gift from his grandparents and had seen a fair amount of usage. But young Peter was done with it, and he wanted to make a dramatic statement. So he invited some friends to witness his break with the Bible and everything within its pages.

The year was 1967. Now, a great number of wild and crazy things happened in the '60s, especially around '67 and '68. A lot of people smoked dope, took LSD, had random sex (which was freely available), demonstrated against the war, and took over college classrooms. All of that was pretty much par for the course in the '60s. It was a time of anarchy, chaos, and rebellion. Flags were burned and bras were burned. But I must confess that I had never come across anyone who had rebelled by burning a Bible. That was a first for me.

Hitchens tells the story in his own words. And please note that
this is not Christopher Hitchens, the well-known atheist. This is
Peter Hitchens, a popular columnist, author, war correspondent, and
the younger brother of Christopher.

> The [Bible] did not, as I had hoped, blaze fiercely
> and swiftly. Only after much blowing and encour-
> agement did I manage to get it to ignite at all, and
> I was left with a disagreeable, half-charred mess.
> Most of my small invited audience drifted away
> long before I had finished, disappointed by the
> anticlimax and the pettiness of the thing. Thunder
> did not mutter. It would be many years before I
> would feel a slight shiver of unease about my act of
> desecration. Did I then have any idea of the forces
> I was trifling with?
>
> I was engaged at the time in a full, perfect, and
> complete rebellion against everything I had been
> brought up to believe. Since I had been raised to be
> an English gentleman, this was quite an involved
> process. It included behaving more or less like a
> juvenile delinquent, trying to look like a walking
> mountain range, using as much foul language as
> I could find excuse for, mocking the weak (such
> as a wheelchair-bound boy in my class who pro-
> vided a specially shameful target for this impulse),
> insulting my elders, and eventually breaking the
> law. I haughtily scorned those adults who, out of

alarm, concern, love, or duty, sought to warn me or restrain me. Nobody can say I did not take my new anti-beliefs to their logical conclusions—hence the decision to finish the job and outrage my religious upbringing by incinerating Holy Writ.[1]

Years later, something happened to Peter Hitchens that he did not foresee the day he tried to burn the pages of his Bible.

He became a Christian.

In his book *The Rage Against God: How Atheism Led Me to Faith*, he relates the remarkable path that ultimately led to his conversion to Christ. While he doesn't spend much time in his story rehashing his past sins, he does give enough information about his behavior to make something perfectly clear.

He had to learn the hard way.

A few years ago one of my sons introduced me to one of his friends from church. I hadn't seen this young man since he was in high school with my son, and he was now closing in on thirty. I knew that he had taken some paths that had caused much pain not only to himself but also to his family. But as with Peter Hitchens, the hound of heaven had relentlessly pursued him. He had recently turned to the Lord with his whole heart, and his life was in the process of much repair and healing. Within the first sixty seconds of our conversation, he alluded to his past and said with downcast eyes, "I guess I had to learn the hard way."

I put my hand on his shoulder, made eye contact with him, and said, "We all learn the hard way. I've never met anyone who learned the easy way."

We all have different stories and foolish decisions in our past. Some have lived out their rebellion in more dramatic ways than others—but we are all rebels at heart. That's why we all have to learn the hard way.

Some, however, have a harder path than others.

THE UNIVERSITY OF AFFLICTION

As a young man, John Newton was the chief of rebels and hell-raisers in the British navy. He was such a blasphemer that other sailors didn't want to get near him, fearing they might be caught up along with him someday when God decided to strike him dead. God broke Newton, who eventually became a captain of slave ships, when he himself was taken captive and made a slave along the coast of Africa.

It's ironic that this white Englishman who transported black slaves from Africa himself became a slave in Africa. And his master was a black woman who was the mistress of a white slave trader. This woman chained him, humiliated him, and starved him to the point that Newton would pull roots out of the ground and eat them unwashed and raw. The other black slaves felt him to be so mistreated that in the middle of the night they brought him food out of their own meager rations.[2]

At the age of twenty-one, Newton's rebellious spirit began to break. But it didn't happen overnight. For a long time, he continued to resist the hand of God and the lessons of adversity. But finally his foolish and darkened heart called out to Christ for mercy. This young, rebellious hellion was destined to become a great pastor and one of the greatest hymn writers ever known in the body of Christ.

But first he had to undergo a journey from England to Africa. And it was in Africa that he, too, received his university education—in the university of affliction. In his autobiography, Newton wrote: "The dreary coast of Africa was the *university* to which the Lord was pleased to send me, and I dare not acknowledge a relation to any other."[3]

After Newton was released from slavery, his heart actually began to grow hard again. Months later, as he was sailing on a ship, a massive storm threatened to crush the vessel and its entire crew. Newton worked the pumps for nine hours straight, then took an hour to rest, and then worked the pumps for another twelve hours without relief.[4] For the first time since he was a young boy, he began to pray. His heart was beginning to slightly soften, but many more difficult days were ahead for the willful and obstinate young man.

He, too, was going learn the hard way.

Of all of the men in history who have learned the lessons of life the hard way, there is no more extreme example than King Nebuchadnezzar of Babylon. This man in his day was head of the most powerful nation on the face of the earth. He had limitless authority—the law was whatever he said it was. He owned nations the way a ten-year-old owns baseball cards. He was a pagan and worshipper of false gods, but on two occasions he had direct, dramatic encounters with the greatness and power of Daniel's God.

While he acknowledged God's greatness, he was still not yet ready to bend his knee and submit to the one true God. He was still taken by his own personal greatness and authority. He bowed to nothing except his own ego.

But all of that was about to change.

The historical account in Daniel 4 is one of the most astonishing in the entire Bible on the power and sovereignty of God over human kings and political leaders. In times of tyranny it is a great comfort to read of indescribable greatness of God over the so-called powerful men of earth. In reality they are ants—they are worms—we might even say that they are slugs, so great is their utter insignificance to the only true God and His Son. This true story of what God did to teach His greatness to Nebuchadnezzar is beyond incredible.

Do the words *flummoxed* and *flabbergasted* come to mind?

The king of Babylon had refused to acknowledge God's greatness over his own ... and that's why he had to learn the hard way.

Just like the rest of us.

HIGH TUITION

Why do we have to learn the hard way? It can be reduced down to *pride*. Pride is the oil spill that just keeps pumping out of our hearts and ruining everything. Pride is about our glory instead of God's, and it puts us on the throne instead of the Lord Jesus. Pride is all about calling the shots in your life, so that you can be better than everyone else. No one has defined it better than C. S. Lewis in *Mere*

Christianity. The following comes from the chapter entitled "The Great Sin":

> According to Christian teachers, the essential vice, the utmost evil, is Pride. Unchastity, anger, greed, drunkenness, and all that, are mere fleabites in comparison: it was through Pride that the devil became the devil: Pride leads to every other vice; it is the complete anti-God state of mind.... Pride gets no pleasure out of having something, only out of having it more than the next man. We say that people are proud of being rich, or clever, or better-looking than others. If everyone else became equally rich, or clever, or good-looking there would be nothing to be proud about. It is the comparison that makes you proud: the pleasure of being above the rest....
>
> In God you come up against something which is in every respect immeasurably superior to yourself. Unless you know God as that—and therefore know yourself as nothing in comparison—you do not know God at all. As long as you are proud you cannot know God. A proud man is always looking down on things and people: and, of course, as long as you are looking down, you cannot see something that is above you.[5]

I think that explains Psalm 14:1–3:

The fool says in his heart, "There is no God." They are corrupt, they do abominable deeds, there is none who does good.

The LORD looks down from heaven on the children of man, to see if there are any who understand, who seek after God.

They have all turned aside; together they have become corrupt; there is none who does good, not even one.

Why is it that no one seeks God?

It's because of pride.

Notice that God is looking down, but men aren't looking up. Why aren't they looking up? Because they want to be kings of their own lives, looking down on others and putting themselves first. That's why no one seeks God on his own, apart from the working of God's Spirit.

NEBUCHADNEZZAR'S TIP-OFF

I'm sure you've had the experience of looking forward to seeing a movie and then having a friend blurt out the ending to you. There's nothing worse than someone spoiling a good movie or book by telling you how it ends. That's precisely what Nebuchadnezzar did at the beginning of Daniel 4. He didn't tell the whole story at all, but he said just enough to let you know that he had experienced a major change of heart:

> King Nebuchadnezzar to all peoples, nations, and
> languages, that dwell in all the earth: Peace be mul-
> tiplied to you! It has seemed good to me to show
> the signs and wonders that the Most High God has
> done for me. How great are his signs, how mighty
> his wonders! His kingdom is an everlasting king-
> dom, and his dominion endures from generation to
> generation. (Dan. 4:1–3)

What an email this was! Note that he copied everyone in the whole world. He wanted every person on the globe to understand the cataclysmic things that had just happened to him.

Beginning in verse 2, he stated that he was writing to let everyone under his rule and reign know "the signs and wonders that the Most High God has done for me."

That sounds like a personal testimony to me.

When I was a kid growing up in church, sometimes at Sunday-night service the pastor would get up and say, "Let's take a few minutes to hear what the Lord has done in your life this week. Who's got a testimony they can share tonight about God's work in your life?" And then someone would get up and give a brief account of an answer to prayer or a providential opportunity to share the gospel that occurred at a restaurant.

That's what Nebuchadnezzar is doing. But he's not going to do it in two minutes, because he's the king. In fact, he will take a whole chapter to tell the amazing story.

And guess what? It begins with another dream.

Nebuchadnezzar's Tree

I, Nebuchadnezzar, was at ease in my house and
flourishing in my palace. I saw a dream and it
made me fearful; and these fantasies as I lay on
my bed and the visions in my mind kept alarming
me. So I gave orders to bring into my presence all
the wise men of Babylon, that they might make
known to me the interpretation of the dream.
Then the magicians, the conjurers, the Chaldeans
and the diviners came in and I related the dream
to them, but they could not make its interpretation known to me. But finally Daniel came in
before me, whose name is Belteshazzar according
to the name of my god, and in whom is a spirit of
the holy gods; and I related the dream to him, saying, "O Belteshazzar, chief of the magicians, since
I know that a spirit of the holy gods is in you and
no mystery baffles you, tell me the visions of my
dream which I have seen, along with its interpretation. Now these were the visions in my mind as I
lay on my bed: I was looking, and behold, there
was a tree in the midst of the earth and its height
was great. The tree grew large and became strong
and its height reached to the sky, and it was visible to the end of the whole earth. Its foliage was
beautiful and its fruit abundant, and in it was food
for all. The beasts of the field found shade under

it, and the birds of the sky dwelt in its branches, and all living creatures fed themselves from it.

"I was looking in the visions in my mind as I lay on my bed, and behold, an angelic watcher, a holy one, descended from heaven. He shouted out and spoke as follows: 'Chop down the tree and cut off its branches, strip off its foliage and scatter its fruit; let the beasts flee from under it and the birds from its branches. Yet leave the stump with its roots in the ground, but with a band of iron and bronze around it in the new grass of the field; and let him be drenched with the dew of heaven, and let him share with the beasts in the grass of the earth. Let his mind be changed from that of a man and let a beast's mind be given to him, and let seven periods of time pass over him. This sentence is by the decree of the angelic watchers and the decision is a command of the holy ones, in order that the living may know that the Most High is ruler over the realm of mankind, and bestows it on whom He wishes and sets over it the lowliest of men.'

"This is the dream which I, King Nebuchadnezzar, have seen. Now you, Belteshazzar, tell me its interpretation, inasmuch as none of the wise men of my kingdom is able to make known to me the interpretation; but you are able, for a spirit of the holy gods is in you." (Dan. 4:4–18 NASB)

Many biblical scholars believe that the dream described here in chapter 4 took place about thirty years after Shadrach, Meshach, and Abednego were delivered from the fiery furnace. The reason they think so is because verse 30 (which we will soon see) speaks of all of the king's vast building projects being completed when he had this dream.

And if nothing else, Nebuchadnezzar was a builder.

He would knock out a Disney World or SeaWorld complex about every two years. He was the one who built the hanging gardens of Babylon, which was one of the Seven Wonders of the World. But by the time Daniel 4 rolled around, he was getting up there in years, and the building projects were over. That's when this dream about a tree hit him in 3-D and Technicolor. And once again, as he did over three decades before, he wanted Daniel to interpret the dream for him.

But Daniel had a problem with that dream. It was obviously a divine preview of coming attractions, and those attractions weren't very attractive.

DANIEL'S TRANSLATION

> Then Daniel, whose name is Belteshazzar, was appalled for a while as his thoughts alarmed him. The king responded and said, "Belteshazzar, do not let the dream or its interpretation alarm you." Belteshazzar replied, "My lord, if only the dream

applied to those who hate you and its interpretation
to your adversaries!

"The tree that you saw, which became large
and grew strong, whose height reached to the sky
and was visible to all the earth and whose foliage
was beautiful and its fruit abundant, and in which
was food for all, under which the beasts of the field
dwelt and in whose branches the birds of the sky
lodged—it is you, O king; for you have become great
and grown strong, and your majesty has become
great and reached to the sky and your dominion to
the end of the earth. In that the king saw an angelic
watcher, a holy one, descending from heaven and
saying, 'Chop down the tree and destroy it; yet
leave the stump with its roots in the ground, but
with a band of iron and bronze around it in the new
grass of the field, and let him be drenched with the
dew of heaven, and let him share with the beasts
of the field until seven periods of time pass over
him,' this is the interpretation, O king, and this is
the decree of the Most High, which has come upon
my lord the king: that you be driven away from
mankind and your dwelling place be with the beasts
of the field, and you be given grass to eat like cattle
and be drenched with the dew of heaven; and seven
periods of time will pass over you, until you recognize that the Most High is ruler over the realm of
mankind and bestows it on whomever He wishes.

And in that it was commanded to leave the stump with the roots of the tree, your kingdom will be assured to you after you recognize that it is Heaven that rules.

"Therefore, O king, may my advice be pleasing to you: break away now from your sins by doing righteousness and from your iniquities by showing mercy to the poor, in case there may be a prolonging of your prosperity." (Dan. 4:19–27 NASB)

Give Daniel full credit—he had the guts to tell the king what he didn't want to hear. Daniel was a man of God, and men of God deliver the message of God—regardless of its content. This reminds me of the great prophet Micaiah in 2 Chronicles 18. Jehoshaphat, king of Judah, was a pretty good king, but he'd made a bad deal with a bad king.

The bad king was Ahab, king of Israel and one of the wickedest kings in the Old Testament. Ahab had conned Jehoshaphat into going to war with him against the Syrians. Prior to the battle, Ahab's phony prophets told the two kings that they would achieve victory, but Jehoshaphat wasn't completely buying it. He asked Ahab if there were any prophets of the Lord available. Ahab brought up Micaiah but indicated that he wasn't real high on him because he never prophesied good about him. Jehoshaphat wanted to hear what Micaiah had to say, so they sent a messenger to get him.

The messenger asked Micaiah to say something good to Ahab. Micaiah's reply was classic in 2 Chronicles 18:13: "As the LORD lives, what my God says, that I will speak."

Don't blow right by those words.

It took a lot of courage for Micaiah to stand up for his faith.

It isn't easy to speak God's words before your colleagues at work, your neighbor down the street, or the kids at school, let alone before a proud, all-powerful monarch—especially one who has little interest in obeying the Lord. Micaiah had courage and so did Daniel. I like the words of G. K. Chesterton:

> Courage is almost a contradiction in terms. It means a strong desire to live taking the form of a readiness to die.... This paradox is the whole principle of courage; even of quite earthly or quite brutal courage. A man cut off by the sea may save his life if he will risk it on the precipice. He can only get away from death by continually stepping within an inch of it. A soldier surrounded by enemies, if he is to cut his way out, needs to combine a strong desire for living with a strange carelessness about dying. He must not merely cling to life, for then he will be a coward, and will not escape. He must not merely wait for death, for then he will be a suicide, and will not escape. He must seek his life in a spirit of furious indifference to it; he must desire life like water and yet drink death like wine.[6]

It was John Trapp who said, "Truth must be spoken however it is taken." Now here's the deal. Daniel had the courage to tell Nebuchadnezzar the truth—but Nebuchadnezzar didn't have the courage to repent. He chose to stay in his sin and to keep himself on the throne of his life. He might have been a little nervous for a few days as he pondered Daniel's message. But he shook off God's warning like an ankle sprain. Actually he walked away from the warning. He was just too proud to give in to the one true God.

Days turned into weeks and weeks turned into months, and he was still okay. Maybe he wondered in the back of his mind whether the wise and insightful Daniel had slipped just a little, making predictions that hadn't come true. What the king didn't realize was that God's clock was still ticking. And it went off like a time bomb twelve months later.

TIME'S UP

All this happened to Nebuchadnezzar the king. Twelve months later he was walking on the roof of the royal palace of Babylon. The king reflected and said, "Is this not Babylon the great, which I myself have built as a royal residence by the might of my power and for the glory of my majesty?" While the word was in the king's mouth, a voice came from heaven, saying, "King Nebuchadnezzar, to you it is declared: sovereignty has been removed from you, and you will be driven away from mankind, and your dwelling place will be with the beasts of the field. You will be given grass to eat like cattle, and seven periods of time will pass over you until you recognize that the Most High is ruler over the realm of mankind and bestows it on whomever He wishes." Immediately the word concerning Nebuchadnezzar was fulfilled; and he was driven away from mankind and began eating grass like cattle, and his body was drenched with the dew of heaven until his hair had grown like eagles' feathers and his nails like birds' claws. (vv. 28–33 NASB)

Nebuchadnezzar was walking and pondering all of his great achievements and accomplishments when suddenly a voice rang out that chilled him to the bone. Sovereignty had been removed from him and so had his mind. He would now live as an animal instead of a king. He would graze with Angus for the next seven years. And then his mind would be restored to him. In that process, he was going to learn who was great and who was to be worshipped. But because of his pride, he was going to learn the hard way.

When the verdict was rendered, it was immediately executed. The New York lawyers couldn't help Nebuchadnezzar, and he couldn't file an appeal. A sympathetic media couldn't wallpaper over the situation with deceptive words and let the king slip out the back door.

God had spoken.

And when He moves, He moves swiftly.

Nebuchadnezzar had had his opportunity, but it passed him by. Now it was time to serve the sentence.

His mind was taken from him and so was his pride and dignity. It was a high price to pay.

NEBUCHADNEZZAR'S TURNAROUND

> But at the end of that period, I, Nebuchadnezzar,
> raised my eyes toward heaven and my reason
> returned to me, and I blessed the Most High and
> praised and honored Him who lives forever; for
> His dominion is an everlasting dominion, and His
> kingdom endures from generation to generation.
> All the inhabitants of the earth are accounted as
> nothing, but He does according to His will in
> the host of heaven and among the inhabitants of
> earth; and no one can ward off His hand or say
> to Him, "What have You done?" At that time
> my reason returned to me. And my majesty and
> splendor were restored to me for the glory of
> my kingdom, and my counselors and my nobles
> began seeking me out; so I was reestablished in
> my sovereignty, and surpassing greatness was
> added to me. Now I, Nebuchadnezzar, praise,
> exalt and honor the King of heaven, for all His
> works are true and His ways just, and He is
> able to humble those who walk in pride. (Dan.
> 4:34–37 NASB)

Nebuchadnezzar emerged from seven years in the pasture glorifying God. That's the mark of a changed man. Thomas Watson said that glorifying God consists of four things: appreciation, adoration, affection, and submission.[7] After this experience, Nebuchadnezzar wasn't strutting around town thumping his gilded suspenders and glorifying himself. No, he was glorifying God. When a man begins to appreciate, adore, and have great affection for God, that's the sign of a man with a changed heart.

But I left out the fourth piece—which is submission. There is a strong note in Nebuchadnezzar's mouth and heart that rings of deep submission to the sovereign God. Nebuchadnezzar has gotten his eyes off his throne and raised them up to God's throne.

At the end of seven years of grazing in the pasture, something happened to Nebuchadnezzar. God healed him. God brought him back to his senses. The last line explains the necessity of those seven long years with the cattle: "[God] is able to humble those who walk in pride." That pretty much sums it up. And we would do well to remember it.

One of the proofs that Nebuchadnezzar was genuinely humbled is also in verse 37. Nebuchadnezzar stated that "all His works are true and His ways just." There's no sense here of resentment or bitterness toward God. He fully accepts what God did to him. He's not questioning the goodness of God, and he's not questioning his seven-year sabbatical of eating grass. It reminds me of what the psalmist said in Psalm 119:71: "It is good for me that I was afflicted." Earlier in Psalm 119:67, he proclaimed, "Before I was afflicted I went astray, but now I keep Your word." And in the very next verse, you find this statement: "You are good, and do good" (NKJV).

No bitterness, no seething resentment, just an acknowledgement that the good and sovereign God took him to the woodshed—and he's a better man for the discipline.

As we get older, we start to figure out that there is a better way than the hard way. The hard way can be avoided when we are open to another way of doing things. Actually I would suggest three ways:

- The teachable way
- The repentant way
- The obedient way

THE TEACHABLE WAY

Psalm 119:9–12 describes the teachable way:

How can a young man keep his way pure?
By keeping it according to Your word.

With all my heart I have sought You;
Do not let me wander from Your commandments.

Your word I have treasured in my heart,
That I may not sin against You.

Blessed are You, O LORD;
Teach me Your statutes. (NASB)

Teachability is a matter of the heart. A teachable heart is neither stubborn nor obstinate, and it refuses to argue with the Creator.

Characterized by a quickness to hear and a propensity to listen, such a heart pays close attention to the Word of God and the promptings of the Spirit of God.

Back in 1969, the Brooklyn Bridge was nearly ninety years old. As David McCullough told the story, some of the hardware on the bridge was beginning to show significant wear, and a young civil engineer was instructed to find the original drawings.

> The "trunnion," as it is called, is a steel joint assembly, or gudgeon, about eighty of which are used to connect the vertical cables of the Brooklyn Bridge to the roadway out at the center of the river span where the greatest movement occurs. It is not an especially complicated or interesting device and it need concern us no longer, but like every other part and piece of the bridge, it had been custom-made to begin with and so could be replaced only by remaking it from scratch. Hence the need for the drawings.[8]

When the young engineer, Francis P. Valentine, was trying to find the drawings, he was told to go to the old carpenters shop on Kent Avenue. He was further advised to wear old clothes, because the place was older than the Brooklyn Bridge and was covered in dirt, dust, and a number of other things. In this old, virtually abandoned shop, he found over ten thousand original blueprints and drawings. Many were signed by Washington Roebling, the engineer who had built the bridge. The various drawings were scattered everywhere.

Some were in file drawers that hadn't been opened in decades, and others were simply strewn across old storage cabinets and bins.

One thing in particular stood out to Valentine, and that was the difference between the blueprints from the 1800s and modern-day blueprints.

> If in a modern drawing, for example, when rivets
> need be shown, a few suffice, the rest are indicated
> by a small *x*, and a marginal note specifies the
> number required. In these from the last century, as
> Frank Valentine likes to point out, "If there were
> 140 rivets in a connection, every rivet was drawn,
> and every one showing how the light would strike
> it." In drawings such as those of the caissons, each
> bolt and brace is shown; even the grain of the wood
> is rendered meticulously in watercolors. In part, but
> only in part, this can be explained by the fact that
> many who worked on the bridge were illiterate, or
> at least so far as reading plans, but as superb crafts-
> men they could build just about anything if it were
> pictured exactly as it was meant to look, exactly as
> it was supposed to be put together.[9]

Now, I have a question for you. These drawings were done in such clear detail that even craftsmen who couldn't read could understand the wishes of the architect. But what if that craftsman wasn't teachable? What if he decided to make his own changes to the architect's plans? What if he decided to ignore the clear instructions of the designer? And multiply that by the hundreds of craftsmen who constructed that bridge. What if they weren't teachable? What would be the practical result? The result would be chaos and a bridge without structural integrity.

The great Brooklyn Bridge could have been a bridge to nowhere.

It's possible for someone to be highly educated but spiritually illiterate. It's possible to read the words of Scripture without a teachable spirit. That is spiritual illiteracy. It's our tendency to read the Word and not apply it. But that must be fought against at all costs. A man or woman without a teachable spirit is doomed—they cannot grow. But with a teachable spirit, the Spirit of God can do mighty things in a person's life—and the lessons don't have to be learned the hard way.

THE REPENTANT WAY

When Daniel told Nebuchadnezzar the meaning of his dream and the severe consequences that God would surely bring his way, he still refused to repent. In fact, he kept putting it off for twelve months. "By delay of repentance, sin strengthens, and the heart hardens. The longer ice freezes the harder it is to be broken," wrote Thomas Watson. During those twelve months, Nebuchadnezzar's heart became harder and harder. But after losing his mind and living with animals for seven years—God put him back in his right mind. But he first had to be broken, because of the hardness of his heart.

The repentant is a heart tender to the things of God, responding quickly to the convictions and reproofs of the Holy Spirit. If God is convicting you of a specific sin, then *deal with it*. Not next week or next month—turn from it and go the other way *now*.

That is the essence of repentance. And it's an easier way.

Just ask Nebuchadnezzar.

THE OBEDIENT WAY

"Judas heard all Christ's sermons."

That's a quote from Thomas Goodwin, and I find it chilling.

Think on that for a moment. Judas heard every sermon our Lord preached. He was an eyewitness of every miracle. But he never obeyed; he never yielded on the inside.

Now let's be clear here. Am I going to obey the Lord all of the time? No. Even though I am in Christ and justified by Him from my sin, sin still dwells within me—and it dwells within you. The apostle Paul described our experience with sin even as he described his own in Romans 7:15–25:

> For what I am doing, I do not understand. For what I will to do, that I do not practice; but what I hate, that I do. If, then, I do what I will not to do, I agree with the law that it is good. But now, it is no longer I who do it, but sin that dwells in me. For I know that in me (that is, in my flesh) nothing good dwells; for to will is present with me, but how to perform what is good I do not find. For the good that I will to do, I do not do; but the evil I will not

to do, that I practice. Now if I do what I will not to
do, it is no longer I who do it, but sin that dwells
in me.

I find then a law, that evil is present with me,
the one who wills to do good. For I delight in the
law of God according to the inward man. But I see
another law in my members, warring against the
law of my mind, and bringing me into captivity to
the law of sin which is in my members. O wretched
man that I am! Who will deliver me from this body
of death? I thank God—through Jesus Christ our
Lord!

So then, with the mind I myself serve the law
of God, but with the flesh the law of sin. (NKJV)

There is a battle to obey because sin still lives in the believer. So
we will fight sin and struggle to obey every day of our lives. Judas
never fought this battle. He wasn't torn over his sin on a daily basis,
because sin was his master. He had never bowed the knee to Christ
in his heart. He never really knew the Lord from his heart of hearts.

If you are trusting in Christ alone to save you and sustain you,
then you will fight this battle of obedience. The words of C. H.
Spurgeon, however, are a great encouragement when we become
worn out in the battle:

If any of you are now disobedient, or have been so,
the road to a better state of things is trust in God.
You cannot hope to render obedience by the more

forcing of conduct into a certain groove, or by a personal, unaided effort of the resolution. There is a free-grace road to obedience, and that is receiving, by faith, the Lord Jesus, who is the gift of God, and is made of God unto us sanctification. We accept the Lord Jesus by faith, and he teaches us obedience, and creates it in us. The more of faith in him you have, the more of obedience to him will you manifest.[10]

The key here is not to make a bunch of resolutions to live a moral life. The key is to call out to the Lord Jesus and ask Him to teach you obedience. And not only ask Him to teach obedience to you but also ask Him to create it in you. He's the Savior and He's the One we want to obey. But we need His help for every breath, every step, every choice, and every obedience.

And what happens if we fall short? He saves us—time and time again.

The fact of the matter is He laid aside His privileges and came to this earth to bear our sins. He took our sins on Himself, suffered horribly, shed His blood, became our substitute, and paid the price for us.

In other words, He came down from heaven and took the hard way ... so we wouldn't have to.

*"The lure of the distant and the difficult is deceptive.
The great opportunity is where you are."*

John Burroughs

Chapter Seven

A SLIGHT THING

In his book *The Mystery of Providence,* John Flavel wrote of a French believer by the name of Du Moulin, who was running for his life from persecutors and climbed into an oven to hide. Within moments a spider began to weave a web over the mouth of the oven. Du Moulin's enemies, seeing the spider's web, never dreamed that he was inside. And thus he was delivered.[1]

For thousands of years, God has been looking out for His people. If He needs to do something extraordinary to provide for them, then so be it. There are many astonishing deliverances recorded in Scripture, but no doubt countless millions of them over the centuries are known only by those who were delivered. Most of the amazing providences of God are neither recorded nor famous. When you think about it, out of all the many, many miracles of the Lord Jesus, we know of just a relative handful. The apostle John made that very clear when he wrote, *"Now there are also many other things that Jesus did. Were every one of them to be written, I suppose that the world itself could not contain the books that would be written"* (John 21:25).

Flavel wrote of another persecuted believer who was hiding for many days from his cutthroat enemies. He dared not leave his hiding place, even to eat. He survived because a hen would lay an egg every day within reach of where he was hiding. Flavel also told of a group of Christians who were near starvation in the coastal town of La Rochelle, France. At their weakest moment, a huge school of fish came right into the harbor, and these starving Christians were fed. He remarked that never before and never since had such an event taken place in that harbor. He then spoke of a Mr. Dodd, who one night in bed had such a strong impression about his neighbor being in danger that he got up, dressed, and went to the man's home. The man answered the knock in the middle of the night, holding the rope with which he was preparing to commit suicide.[2]

You see, God doesn't just deliver men like Daniel, Shadrach, Meshach, and Abednego. He delivers common people like you and me all of the time. God has not stopped delivering His people. He is constantly at work in our lives and in the lives of believers around the world.

Before we get to Daniel and the handwriting on the wall, we need to take a quick look at a deliverance that occurred under the prophet Elisha.

"A SLIGHT THING ..."

Second Kings 3 gives the historical account of King Jehoshaphat and two other kings going up against the army of Moab. The passage points out clearly that they were in terrible trouble because they were in the middle of a drought, and after a week of traveling, ran completely out of water. There was no water to be found anywhere within that raging furnace of a valley, and the army and their animals were about to die of thirst. The streambeds were dry and cracked. It was a hopeless situation and a huge crisis. What a horrific way to die!

And then the prophet Elisha showed up and told them that by the next morning, every stream, every creek, and every pond would be overflowing with water. As a result, they needed to get out their shovels and start digging trenches. But here's the astonishing thing: Elisha said there would be no storm and no rain—and the water would be everywhere.

And the next morning that is exactly what happened. The trenches and creek beds were so filled with water that it was a virtual flood. The men and the animals could drink their fill and not die of thirst. God had delivered them.

But there was one additional aspect to this miracle. The army of Moab saw the sun reflecting off the water and the red sandstone, and it looked to them like blood. They immediately concluded that the three armies had made war with one another, and their blood was running everywhere. So the army of Moab charged in to what they thought was a graveyard … where Jehoshaphat and his allies were waiting in ambush. And not only did God give them water, but He gave their enemies into their hands and they won a crushing victory.

What a spectacular deliverance! According to 2 Kings 3:20, there were flash floods many miles away in the mountains of Edom.[3] The storm wasn't heard, no lightning was observed, and no rain fell where they were. But God used that massive storm miles and miles away to fill the streams where they were dying of thirst.

Just for a moment, let's focus in on a phrase that Elisha used as he told Jehoshaphat about what the Lord was about to do to deliver them (2 Kings 3:16–18 NASB):

> He said, "Thus says the LORD, 'Make this valley full of trenches.'
>
> For thus says the LORD, 'You shall not see wind nor shall you see rain; yet that valley shall be filled with water, so that you shall drink, both you and your cattle and your beasts.
>
> *This is but a slight thing in the sight of the LORD.'"*

In other words: "Seeing your desperate situation, and knowing that you and your livestock are about to die of thirst, here's what the Lord is about to do: Numerous miles away, He will send storms, lightning, and torrential rains that neither you nor your enemies will see or hear. He will then use the resulting flashfloods in the mountains to flow swiftly and silently into this valley, filling every trench, wash, creek, and riverbed to overflowing, in order to quench your thirst. And while He's at it, He will use that same silent flood, illuminated by the red light of dawn, to deceive, defeat, and utterly destroy your enemies. And by the way … this is just a slight thing for the Lord to do. It's no trouble for Him at all. It's really not that big of a deal to Him. He really won't have to even raise His little finger."

It's a slight thing.

It's a small thing.

It's a light thing … for the Lord to do this for you.

It's a slight thing for the Lord to send a spider to hide you, fish in the harbor to feed you, or water to slake your thirst and fool your enemies. It's not a monumental undertaking for the Lord to do any of these things. It's a slight thing—no big deal.

That's how great His power is … the same power that remains abundantly available to those today who find themselves in threatening circumstances.

What are you facing in your life that frightens and intimidates you? Is it some threatening person or threatening situation? Do you feel hemmed in with no way of escape? Are circumstances closing in on you to such a degree that you have lost all peace in your heart?

Know this: It is a slight thing for the Lord to deliver you. He knows all about your situation, and He knows every detail of what threatens, intimidates, depresses, or discourages you. He knows more about it than you do. He has not forgotten you, so do not forget Him. If you are in desperate straits, pray David's prayer of desperation in Psalm 57:2–3: "I will cry to God Most High, to God who accomplished all things for me. He will send from heaven and save me" (NASB).

The power of God is mind-boggling. It's a slight thing for Him to raise up nations or set them down. It's a slight thing for Him to raise up a ruler or take him down. And King Belshazzar, in Daniel 5, was about to get a firsthand demonstration of the power of the one true God whom he had been so quick to mock and ignore.

In fact, there are three lessons for us in Daniel 5 regarding the power of God:

1. It is a slight thing for the Lord to turn the pages of history (vv. 1–4).
2. It is a slight thing for the Lord to bring down a young and arrogant ruler (vv. 5–9).
3. It is a slight thing for the Lord to raise up His man at a critical moment (vv. 10–30).

THE HANDWRITING ON THE WALL
It's a slight thing for the Lord to turn the pages of history.

Belshazzar the king made a great feast for a thousand of his lords, and drank wine in the presence of the thousand. While he tasted the wine, Belshazzar gave the command to bring the gold and silver vessels which his father Nebuchadnezzar had taken from the temple which had been in Jerusalem, that the king and his lords, his wives, and his concubines might drink from them. Then they brought the gold vessels that had been taken from the temple of the house of God which had been in Jerusalem; and the king and his lords, his wives, and his concubines drank from them. They drank wine, and praised the

gods of gold and silver, bronze and iron, wood and
stone. (Dan. 5:1–4 NKJV)

It was like Academy Award night along the red carpet in
Hollywood, with cameras flashing, and gleaming stretch limos pull-
ing up to the curb, one after another.

The great and powerful people of Babylon had gathered for a
glittering, star-studded banquet at the invitation of King Belshazzar.
And I think it's fair to say that not one of those revelers knew that
within mere hours, the Babylonian Empire would cease to exist.

Who could have imagined such a thought? Babylon fall?
Ridiculous thought! This was the mightiest, wealthiest, grandest
empire the world had ever seen and would surely rule the earth for
another thousand years. But even as they binged and purged themselves and drank themselves into oblivion—all of course, in praise of
the gods of gold, silver, bronze, iron, wood, and stone—they were
within hours of being erased from power. The God who made the
gold and silver, bronze, iron, wood, and stone was about to make
His presence known.

This is the first appearance of King Belshazzar in Daniel.
Approximately ten years prior to Belshazzar taking the throne,
Nebuchadnezzar had died after ruling the empire for forty-four
years. Several kings served in the interim, including Belshazzar's
father, Nabonidus. Nabonidus was still alive but was absent from
the kingdom.[4] He had left Babylon to travel extensively (apparently
he couldn't resist those AARP discounts), but before he did, he had
made his oldest son, Belshazzar, king in his place. They were actually

corulers, but with Dad out of town, Belshazzar had the run of the kingdom.

And he wasn't quite up to the task.

He was young, inexperienced, and in over his head.

His father probably assumed that he couldn't do much damage. His son would safely rule from the huge fortress that was the city of Babylon, which was built in a square with each side covering fourteen miles.[5] The north side of the city was fourteen miles, and if you lived on the south side, that was fourteen miles long as well. And if you chose a condo on either the west side or the east side—it was fourteen miles in length either way. It wasn't the kind of town where you could take a stroll around the square after dinner. It was massive—and two huge, impenetrable walls surrounded the sprawling city.

Larry Richards filled in the details:

> The outer wall was 311 feet high, 87 feet thick, and
> 56 miles long. There was a road on top of the wall.
> It was wide enough for six chariots to ride side by
> side. There were 250 towers on top of that wall.
> Each tower was manned by troops. Down below,
> on the outside of the wall, was a canal or moat.
> It surrounded the city and was filled with water.
> People crossed it on drawbridges. Huge gates closed
> off the city. There was a second wall inside the outer
> wall with more soldiers and another road that was
> used for the rapid deployment of troops and sup-
> plies. The river Euphrates flowed under these walls.

It went through the city and out the other side. It provided a constant supply of drinking water.

Several hundred acres of land had been set aside for farming inside the walls. Vegetables and cattle were grown to support the inhabitants of the city. There was enough food and provisions in storage to last for years, and more food could be grown if needed. At the time of Belshazzar's feast, the ever-flowing Euphrates River was full of water, the drawbridges were raised, the gates were closed, sentinels were posted on the walls, and a great army was encroached behind them.[6]

This was a city and an empire that could not be brought down. But here's an interesting fact: As Belshazzar was putting on his great feast, the Medo-Persian army was outside the gates, attempting to take the city. And to show his utter contempt for their efforts to conquer Babylon, Belshazzar threw a party. The enemy was literally outside the gates, but the arrogant young king was so secure in his massive defenses that he didn't consider them to be even a remote threat. There was no way in the world they could get into the city—and yet … that is exactly what would happen within a matter of minutes.

Belshazzar was young and cocky. That's why he specifically sent for the gold and silver drinking vessels that his grandfather Nebuchadnezzar had taken from the temple in Jerusalem. By the way, the text mentions references to Nebuchadnezzar as his "father," but the term can also mean "predecessor." Nebuchadnezzar, his predecessor, had taken the cups from the temple that were to be used exclusively in worshipping and giving glory to the God of Israel. Now this rookie king, with full awareness of their significance, brought them out to celebrate mindless and stupid gods of gold and silver. It was a breathtaking breach for this king to do such a thing. Nebuchadnezzar—for all his pride and swagger—had never done it, and neither had any other king in between. It was nothing short of blasphemy.

This foolish, unqualified, and untested young king gloried in his power and riches. He sat above all of the others and received their adulation and celebrity worship. He didn't know it, but it was all about to come to a screeching halt. That very night God would turn the page of history and bring an end to the once great Babylonian Empire.

It's ironic and providential that God would bring an end to this brash and incompetent young king by using an elderly general to breach the walls. Dr. Gleason Archer wrote of the Medo-Persian general Ugbaru: "Ugbaru was an elderly general who been governor of Gutium; it was he who engineered the capture of Babylon by the stratagem of deflecting the water of the Euphrates into an artificial channel."[7] Some think that God doesn't have a sense of humor, but this surely runs against that mistaken idea. He *invented* humor.

God used an elderly general, who would die within a few weeks of his great victory,[8] to take down a king who had never had a real job in his life—but was intoxicated with his own greatness. The grizzled old general knew there had to be a way in. By diverting the river that ran through the city and marching in through the muddy riverbed and under the walls, he ensured that the incompetent and incapable young king would be dead within hours—and so would his empire.

It's a slight thing for the Lord to bring down a young and arrogant ruler.

> In the same hour the fingers of a man's hand appeared and wrote opposite the lampstand on the plaster of the wall of the king's palace; and the king saw the part of the hand that wrote. Then the king's countenance changed, and his thoughts troubled him, so that the joints of his hips were loosened and his knees knocked against each other. The king cried aloud to bring in the astrologers, the Chaldeans, and the soothsayers. The king spoke, saying to the wise men of Babylon, "Whoever reads this writing, and tells me its interpretation, shall be clothed with purple and have a chain of gold around his neck; and he shall be the third ruler in the kingdom." Now all the king's wise men came, but they could not read the writing, or make known to the king its interpretation. Then King Belshazzar was greatly troubled, his countenance was changed, and his lords were astonished. (Dan. 5:5–9 NKJV)

Stanley Marcus was one of the legendary founders of Neiman Marcus, the upscale department store that he cofounded in Texas.

Neiman Marcus is known for their annual Christmas catalog, which caters to the richest of the rich. Here in Texas, Neiman Marcus is affectionately known as Neiman Mark Up. Stanley Marcus was a brilliant businessman who was known as the ugliest boy in his high school and was constantly the brunt of anti-Semitism. He went to work in his father's small shop and turned it into a retail giant. He worked his way up from rock bottom. In 1986, he wrote these words:

> Thousands of aspiring executives will be gradu-
> ating from the business schools in which the
> management of money has been the central thrust
> of their education.... Their perspective is such
> that they don't want to get behind a sales counter
> to learn about customers or behind a machine to
> learn about products.... Too many young execu-
> tives know something about many things, but not
> a lot about anything. In their race to the presi-
> dency, [they] lose sight of the fact that some jobs
> within a company take years to master.[9]

Marcus was probably describing Belshazzar as well. This foolish and arrogant king was drunk on his own imagined greatness. He thought that nothing could stand in his way. And then he saw the handwriting on the wall of the great banquet hall—and so did the thousand or so guests. Suddenly his mind was redirected from his own greatness to calling 911. His color changed, and his limbs gave way—he couldn't even stand under the fear that was oppressing him and taking away his life-breath. He was absolutely panicked in every sense of the word.

Hysterically, with a loud voice and knocking knees, he screamed for the interpretation specialists. The problem was they were as terrified as he was. Here was this mighty hand, writing on this massive wall. There was no arm, no elbow, no shoulder—just a great hand that had come out of nowhere. In his panic, he offered the third place in the kingdom to whoever could do the job—but none of them were qualified for the task, despite their advanced degrees.

Russell L. Ackoff was a professor at Wharton business school for many years. Wharton is in the very top tier of business schools in the United States. Ackoff was once asked what the principle achievements of a business school education were. He replied, "The first was to equip students with a vocabulary that enabled them to talk authoritatively about subjects they did not understand."[10]

You've got to give credit to Belshazzar's wise men. They didn't try to con him or smoke him. They never said a word. It was all they could do to keep standing without soiling themselves. They were utterly shot through with paralyzing fear. And none of them had a clue. They were supposed to be the best and the brightest, men of wisdom who could interpret dreams and signs. But their wisdom was severely limited when it came to this Great Hand writing a message on the wall of the great banquet hall. Their wisdom was void and meaningless. They were absolutely flummoxed and flabbergasted by what they saw and literally had nothing to say.

What was needed in this situation was a godly man who understood the things of God.

And that is what's *always* needed.

Some five hundred years after this event, the apostle Paul explained it clearly:

> Yet among the mature we do impart wisdom, although it is not a wisdom of this age or of the rulers of this age, who are doomed to pass away. But we impart a secret and hidden wisdom of God, which God decreed before the ages for our glory. None of the rulers of this age understood this, for if they had, they would not have crucified the Lord of glory. But, as it is written,
>
> > "What no eye has seen, nor ear heard,
> > nor the heart of man imagined,
> > what God has prepared for those who love
> > him"—
>
> these things God has revealed to us through the Spirit. For the Spirit searches everything, even the depths of God. For who knows a person's thoughts except the spirit of that person, which is in him? So also no one comprehends the thoughts of God except the Spirit of God. Now we have received not the spirit of the world, but the Spirit who is from God, that we might understand the things freely given us by God. And we impart this in words not taught by human wisdom but taught by the Spirit, interpreting spiritual truths to those who are spiritual.
>
> The natural person does not accept the things of the Spirit of God, for they are folly to him, and he is

> not able to understand them because they are spiritu-
> ally discerned. The spiritual person judges all things,
> but is himself to be judged by no one. "For who has
> understood the mind of the Lord so as to instruct
> him?" But we have the mind of Christ. (1 Cor. 2:6–16)

This crisis was beyond the wisdom of the young and ambitious king. What was needed was a wise, weathered man who had seen kings come and go. What was needed was a man who had been given the mind of Christ.

It's a slight thing for the Lord to raise up His man at a critical moment.

Daniel was somewhere close to eighty years old when Belshazzar threw his great banquet. Without question, Daniel was in the Babylonian Hall of Fame due to his great service to King Nebuchadnezzar. Since that king's passing, however, Daniel's stock seemed to have fallen with Babylon's intelligentsia. His deeds and his counsel had fallen out of favor. In short, as far as the kingdom's current crop of young rulers was concerned, he was yesterday's news.

Maybe so. But Daniel was still alive and had apparently lost nothing of his razor-edged sharpness. God had him waiting in the wings for such a time as this—and he hadn't lost an ounce of True Courage to deliver the message.

> The queen, because of the words of the king and his
> lords, came to the banquet hall. The queen spoke,

saying, "O king, live forever! Do not let your thoughts
trouble you, nor let your countenance change. There
is a man in your kingdom in whom is the Spirit of the
Holy God. And in the days of your father, light and
understanding and wisdom, like the wisdom of the
gods, were found in him; and King Nebuchadnezzar
your father—your father the king—made him chief
of the magicians, astrologers, Chaldeans, and sooth-
sayers. Inasmuch as an excellent spirit, knowledge,
understanding, interpreting dreams, solving riddles,
and explaining enigmas were found in this Daniel,
whom the king named Belteshazzar, now let Daniel
be called, and he will give the interpretation." (Dan.
5:10–12 NKJV)

It's apparent that some time after the death of Nebuchadnezzar,
Daniel took a step back from his previous position of influence. Perhaps
Belshazzar and his young bucks thought that qualified them to put all
of their management theories into practice. But all of their degrees and
SAT scores were forgotten the second they saw the handwriting on the
wall. The queen mother, who more than likely was Nebuchadnezzar's
daughter and Belshazzar's mother, stepped up and immediately named
Daniel as the man who would come through in the clutch.

And isn't it interesting? After all those years, the prophet's real
name has come back to him. The queen refers to him twice as
"Daniel" or "God is my judge."

Daniel is summoned by Belshazzar, who immediately offers him
the third seat of power in his kingdom.

> Then Daniel was brought in before the king. The
> king spoke, and said to Daniel, "Are you that Daniel
> who is one of the captives from Judah, whom my
> father the king brought from Judah? I have heard of
> you, that the Spirit of God is in you, and that light
> and understanding and excellent wisdom are found
> in you. Now the wise men, the astrologers, have
> been brought in before me, that they should read
> this writing and make known to me its interpreta-
> tion, but they could not give the interpretation of
> the thing. And I have heard of you, that you can
> give interpretations and explain enigmas. Now if
> you can read the writing and make known to me its
> interpretation, you shall be clothed with purple and
> have a chain of gold around your neck, and shall
> be the third ruler in the kingdom." (Dan. 5:13–16
> NKJV)

It took Daniel about ten seconds to put this little runt in his place. And then he immediately went to work, delivering God's message. Daniel began with a quick history lesson concerning Nebuchadnezzar and then told the young king that he was account-able for his sin, because he had full knowledge of what God did in his predecessor's life; therefore, the king was responsible for blaspheming the one true God.

> Then Daniel answered, and said before the king,
> "Let your gifts be for yourself, and give your rewards

to another; yet I will read the writing to the king, and make known to him the interpretation. O king, the Most High God gave Nebuchadnezzar your father a kingdom and majesty, glory and honor. And because of the majesty that He gave him, all peoples, nations, and languages trembled and feared before him. Whomever he wished, he executed; whomever he wished, he kept alive; whomever he wished, he set up; and whomever he wished, he put down. But when his heart was lifted up, and his spirit was hardened in pride, he was deposed from his kingly throne, and they took his glory from him. Then he was driven from the sons of men, his heart was made like the beasts, and his dwelling was with the wild donkeys. They fed him with grass like oxen, and his body was wet with the dew of heaven, till he knew that the Most High God rules in the kingdom of men, and appoints over it whomever He chooses.

"But you his son, Belshazzar, have not humbled your heart, although you knew all this. And you have lifted yourself up against the Lord of heaven. They have brought the vessels of His house before you, and you and your lords, your wives and your concubines, have drunk wine from them. And you have praised the gods of silver and gold, bronze and iron, wood and stone, which do not see or hear or know; and the God who holds your breath in His hand and owns all your ways, you have not glorified." (Dan. 5:17–23 NKJV)

And then Daniel delivered the knockout blow that the Great Hand wrote on the wall before the thousand drunken diplomats:

> Then the fingers of the hand were sent from Him, and this writing was written.
> "And this is the inscription that was written: MENE, MENE, TEKEL, UPHARSIN.
> This is the interpretation of each word. MENE: God has numbered your kingdom, and finished it; TEKEK: You have been weighed in the balances, and found wanting; PERES: Your kingdom has been divided, and given to the Medes and Persians." Then Belshazzar gave the command, and they clothed Daniel with purple and put a chain of gold around his neck, and made a proclamation concerning him that he should be the third ruler in the kingdom. (Dan. 5:24–31 NKJV)

In this story, we find two truths that have ready application to our lives and the days in which we live.

TWO TIMELESS TRUTHS

First, God always has His leader prepared and ready for the day of crisis.

When crisis occurs, whether it's in a home, a place of work, or in a nation, what is desperately needed is leadership that is wise, tested, and sure. That only comes from a person who has been quietly prepared for that particular hour.

When I was a kid, my dad did a radio program on Sunday nights. He was on a 50,000-watt station that covered the western United States. It was an hour-long program where my dad would primarily play Christian music and make a few comments here and there between the songs. I would often go into the studio and sit next to him as he would do the program. As soon as his program was over, *The Hour of Decision* with Billy Graham would come on. I can't remember how many times I heard Cliff Barrows introduce Mr. Graham as "God's man for this hour."

God may be preparing you to be his man in a coming hour this very week. It may be that your family is in crisis and a dad or mom needs to step up to the plate. Or perhaps there's a situation brewing at work that requires great wisdom to navigate the difficulty, and the Lord will use you to speak a right word at the right time. Don't be fearful of what you should say in the moment if it suddenly comes up. The Lord told His disciples that in a time to come they would be delivered up to courts and kings that would persecute them. But he also said in Matthew 10 that they should not be worried ahead of time about what to say in such a pressure-packed circumstance: "When they deliver you over, do not be anxious how you are to speak or what you are to say, for what you are to say will be given to you in that hour" (v. 19).

As Daniel needed the mind of Christ for his crisis, so our Lord will give you *His* mind for *your* crisis.

You may not be facing a situation of outright persecution at the moment. And yet you may find yourself anticipating a circumstance where you need to think and speak clearly. You can count on the Lord to give what you need in that moment. Do you have a critical test or exam coming up this week? Then study hard—don't play games. Get your work done and study. And then trust Him to bring to your mind what you studied at the moment you need it.

It's a slight thing for Him to do—and He knows that you need Him to come through in the clutch for you.

Second, God always has a plan in place to replace human failure.

Nebuchadnezzar had finally humbled himself before the Lord after seven years in the alfalfa with the Angus. But young king Belshazzar blew off the life and testimony of Nebuchadnezzar, scorning the lessons of history, utterly refusing to humble himself before God. He failed as a king to lead the people in worship of the one true God. Yet God always has His plan in place. He has already written the next chapter, and human failure cannot thwart His plan.

My friend David Jeremiah wrote about a great story that happened to his friend Robert Morgan not too many years ago.

> My friend Robert Morgan flew into New Orleans several years ago, and the man who met him at the airport was a geophysicist for a major oil company. Driving to the hotel, he explained to Robert that oil deposits result from the decomposition of plant and animal life now buried by eons of time. Oil is found all over the world, he said, even under the

ice of the Arctic and Antarctic. That means forests and abundant vegetation once covered the world until destroyed in a vast global cataclysm (such as a worldwide flood).

The geophysicist went on to say that the earth's richest, deepest, and largest deposits of petroleum lie under the sands of countries just to the east of Israel in the location pinpointed in the Bible as the garden of Eden. Eden was a teeming expanse or forests, foliage, and gardens with rich fertility unparalleled in human history.

Barren sand and blazing desert now exist where once grew a garden flourishing with dense, lush flora, the likes of which the world has not seen since. It was destroyed in some disastrous upheaval and has decayed into the largest deposit of oil in the world. I had never before imagined that the gasoline I pump into my car might be the ruined remains of the rich, vast foliage of the garden of Eden.[11]

The greatest human failure in history was Adam and Eve's rebellion against God. Yet our God always has a plan in place to replace human failure. Romans 5 tells us that the Lord Jesus Christ is the second Adam, and by His sinless life and death He has taken our sin upon Him. He died for us in our place and made it possible for us to be in right relationship with God the Father. Our sins can be forgiven because of what He has done. And one day He will return to set up His kingdom.

In the interim, His plan for the ages marches on, with everything on schedule. The nations of the world fight and battle over oil—black gold—which is the currency of the world. It is remarkable that the oil and gasoline that is refined from it could indeed have come from that garden where Adam and Eve once walked and failed. If indeed the gasoline in your tank is residue from the garden of Eden, we should not be shocked—*it was a slight thing for the Lord to do.*

Just think about that for a few minutes when your difficulties and circumstances seem "too big to handle."

"Inevitably, sooner or later, there comes a crisis ... in which we are brought to the appalling sense of our own ... weakness. That is a great hour."

G. Campbell Morgan

Chapter Eight

IN THE COMPANY OF LIONS

The real reason that Daniel was in the lions' den is very clear.

Apparently the king signed the bill before he read it. Perhaps by the time the bill actually got to his desk, it was close to two thousand pages. The king wouldn't know what was in it until he passed it. So he signed it.

That's it.

But I've already gotten ahead of the story.

Chances are, you already know the story. Just about everyone has heard about Daniel's time in the lions' den. But it's more than just a story. It is historical fact.

Why do you think that the Lord included this particular event out of Daniel's life in the book of Daniel? Why did the actual event happen in the first place? In speaking of the Old Testament and the historical events recorded in its pages, we should take note of Romans 15:4: *"For whatever was written in former days was written for our instruction, that through endurance and through the encouragement of the Scriptures we might have hope."*

Here's what I surmise from that verse, specifically in regard to the historical account of Daniel 6, where Daniel finds himself thrown in a den of lions simply because he refuses to compromise his convictions. At some point in your life, you're going to find yourself in the same kind of situation. You will come to a place where you'll have to decide if you're going to stand for Jesus Christ.

And if you do, you will be surrounded by lions.

Now I grant to you that the lions we face today may be different kinds of lions than those that spent the night with Daniel. But they are lions nonetheless, because they have power to do us great harm.

If you look at the Romans 15:4 reference carefully, it gives the reason why we study the Old Testament and the lives of the godly men and women who lived back in those times. The Old Testament was written for our instruction—and through that instruction of the Scriptures we will gain three things: endurance, encouragement, and hope.

No one knows for sure what's coming in our nation and our world, but I think most of us would say it doesn't look much like the good old days.

It looks more like bad hard days.

And if that's the prospect for the days ahead of us, then what are we going to need? We're going to need endurance, encouragement, and hope. When you've got those three running through your life like a threefold cord, then you've got True Courage.

And how do I get those things in my life? One way is by reading about the faithfulness of God in the Old Testament in the lives of men and women like Daniel, Joseph, Esther, and so many others. That's why we've been looking at Daniel's life so closely. If God gave Daniel what he needed to get through tough days of living under successive kings and tyrants, then won't the Lord do the same for us? Yes, He will. So take heart and take courage. In His providence, God included Daniel's story to give us the spiritual guts to be faithful, to stand strong, and to occupy until He returns.

FAMILIAR STORIES

Sometimes a story is so well known that within the first sentence or two, we're familiar with the beginning, middle, and end. Here's one for you. It might be interesting to see how quickly you can figure it out. In the book *The Wreck of the Titan*, Morgan Robertson told the story of the largest luxury liner ever constructed. The massive ship was over eight hundred feet long and carried a crew of over three thousand. It was an engineering marvel and had so many watertight compartments that it was considered unsinkable.

Because the ship's designers were so confident in its invulnerability, only the minimum number of lifeboats was carried on board. There weren't enough lifeboats for all of the passengers, because, well, they would never be needed. This great ship could not sink.

As the mammoth liner carried its many wealthy passengers across the North Atlantic on its maiden voyage, the unthinkable occurred. The great ship collided with an iceberg just before midnight on a freezing April night in the North Atlantic.

You figured this one out pretty quickly, didn't you? It's obviously the story of the *Titanic*, the great ocean liner that sank in frigid waters after hitting an iceberg. The tragic sinking of the *Titanic* took place on the night of April 14, 1912.

But the story that I am referring to is *not* about the *Titanic*.

The Wreck of the Titan was actually a novel written in 1898, fourteen years before the sinking of the *Titanic*.[1]

So how do you explain something like that? Most people call it a coincidence, but in actuality it is the providence of God at work. As the Westminster Confession of Faith states, "God, the great Creator of all things, doth uphold, direct, dispose, and govern all creatures, actions, and things, from the greatest even to the least." All things from the greatest to the least include novels written fourteen years before the sinking of the *Titanic*.

In my opinion, if we listen well to Daniel 6, we will hear God telling us that one day we will face the lions as Daniel did. The circumstances will be different, and the lions might not have shaggy manes and throaty growls, but they will be lions nonetheless.

Oh, and here's the other thing. It always take True Courage to stand up and face the lions—especially when everything within you is telling you to run. God's sons and daughters don't run from the lions. They face them.

And what is it that will enable you to face such lions?

It will be your confidence in the greatness of the Lord Jesus Christ.

In Revelation 5:5, the Lord is described as "the Lion of the tribe of Judah." Judah was His tribe of origin. Judah was one of Jacob's twelve sons, and when Jacob blessed Judah, he gave him leadership over his brothers (Gen. 49:8–12). In addition, verse 10 indicates that one of Judah's descendants would be worthy of the obedience of all peoples. That is a reference to the Lord Jesus Christ—so there's your explanation of the Lion of Judah. And because He is the Lion of Judah, that means He is the Lion of lions. He created the lions, and He controls them, no matter what shape they may take. Some of them hang out in jungles and zoos, and others wear pinstriped suits, carry briefcases, and file briefs against religious liberty and free speech.

No matter who these beasts are or where they may be found, Jesus is still the Sovereign King and the Lion of lions. And He alone is the source of True Courage to those who trust Him with their whole hearts.

Daniel 6 isn't really about Daniel in the lions' den. It's about the Lion of lions whom Daniel knows and trusts with his whole life.

The Lion of lions rules over bureaucrats (Dan. 6:1–3).

> It pleased Darius to set over the kingdom 120 satraps, to be throughout the whole kingdom; and over them three presidents, of whom Daniel was one, to whom these satraps should give account, so that the king might suffer no loss. Then this Daniel became distinguished above all the other presidents and satraps, because an excellent spirit was in him. And the king planned to set him over the whole kingdom.

Remember the previous chapter when Belshazzar threw his last big party and then was killed as the special forces of the Medes and Persians made their way into the palace? That was Daniel 5, and the

last two verses describe a swift shift in administrations. In verses 30–31
we read: "That very night Belshazzar the Chaldean king was killed.
And Darius the Mede received the kingdom, being about sixty-two
years old."

Let's make two observations here about what has happened.
Quickly following the handwriting on the wall, Daniel had to adjust
to two huge new realities in his life: a new king and a new empire.

Darius the Mede was the new king, and the new empire was the
Medo-Persian Empire. They were the guys who were outside the wall
trying to find a way in when Belshazzar was impressing all of the
beautiful people with how great a king he was. But as we discovered,
the Medo-Persian Navy SEALs got in under the wall by diverting the
river and crashed Belshazzar's party forever.

I'm not going to take much time on this, but there is some
debate among biblical scholars over just who this "Darius the Mede"
really was.

It appears that *Darius* is actually a term for a king, much as
the Romans would call their emperors "Caesar." It seems that this
King Darius was actually a man by the name of Gubaru, who "is
often referred to in tablets dating from 535 to 525 as the governor of
Babylon."[2] The overall king of the Medo-Persian Empire was Cyrus;
but it seems that at this time he was off fighting on another front.
So he appointed Gubaru as king/governor of Babylon while he was
away, but promised to stay in touch by texting frequently. Gubaru is
not Ugbaru—he was the elderly general who diverted the river and
led the SEALs in through the riverbed under the walls.

So you've got to pay attention here. Ugbaru and Gubaru were
not Saddam Hussein's two sons.

All of that to say, Daniel now found himself serving under a new king and new empire. But as far as that was concerned, it didn't affect Daniel much at all—except to give him even greater influence and favor in this new empire.

In a sense, the whole world changed the night that Babylon fell. God shook the earth to its foundations. But since Daniel was protected by God's hand, he went right on serving the Lord as before.

In fact, the new Mede ruler was so impressed with Daniel that he placed him with two other men over the entire kingdom. Daniel, however, was so obviously head-and-shoulders above those other guys that Darius contemplated retiring the other two leaders and promoting Daniel to run the whole kingdom by himself.

The Lion of lions rules over conspiracies (Dan. 6:4–5).

> Then the presidents and the satraps sought to find a ground for complaint against Daniel with regard to the kingdom, but they could find no ground for complaint or any fault, because he was faithful, and no error or fault was found in him. Then these men said, "We shall not find any ground for complaint against this Daniel unless we find it in connection with the law of his God."

Don't imagine, however, that it was all roses and sunshine for Daniel after Babylon fell. Almost immediately he faced an evil conspiracy to undercut and destroy him. As we see from Scripture, the conspirators hired private investigators to dig up dirt on Daniel. But to their consternation, the report came back clean.

His finances were spotless.

He didn't hire prostitutes when he was away on business.

He didn't owe back taxes.

Even his Internet history was clean.

Daniel never had to erase his Internet history, because he had nothing to hide. He wasn't only clean, he was squeaky clean. Mark Twain used to say, "If you tell the truth, you don't have to remember anything." The conspirators tried to bring down Daniel, but they couldn't. He was the real deal—honest, forthright, and aboveboard in all his dealings.

But when did a person's honesty and integrity ever stop someone bent on slander and destruction?

Daniel's story was about to turn again, putting him in deadly danger. However, God was watching over His servant every step of the way as a pack of bureaucratic hyenas tried to bring him down.

The Lion of lions rules over political maneuvering (Dan. 6:6–9).

> Then these presidents and satraps came by agree-
> ment to the king and said to him, "O King Darius,
> live forever! All the presidents of the kingdom,
> the prefects and the satraps, the counselors and

> the governors are agreed that the king should
> establish an ordinance and enforce an injunc-
> tion, that whoever makes petition to any god
> or man for thirty days, except to you, O king,
> shall be cast into the den of lions. Now, O king,
> establish the injunction and sign the document,
> so that it cannot be changed, according to the
> law of the Medes and the Persians, which cannot
> be revoked." Therefore King Darius signed the
> document and injunction.

Things got real dirty real fast.

You might think of it as a backroom deal between the leadership of the House and the Senate to come up with a bill that
would get Daniel out of the way. And the most politically savvy
among them made sure they would present it to the king in such
a way that he would grab the royal pen and sign it into law.

Who knows how they did it. Maybe they told him it was
an emergency and the whole nation was at risk. Maybe they
whispered that the kingdom was too big to fail, and if people
were praying to gods other than the king the whole empire might
go down. At this point, it looked for all the world as if Darius/
Gubaru (or D. G. as his friends called him) signed the bill without reading it.

Whenever that happens, bad things happen.

The bill was probably so full of amendments and grants to universities that the king just didn't have the energy to read it. And little
did he know what he had done to Daniel by his irresponsibility.

The Lion of lions rules over Daniel (Dan. 6:10–15).

When Daniel knew that the document had been
signed, he went to his house where he had windows
in his upper chamber open toward Jerusalem. He
got down on his knees three times a day and prayed
and gave thanks before his God, as he had done
previously. Then these men came by agreement and
found Daniel making petition and plea before his
God. Then they came near and said before the king,
concerning the injunction, "O king! Did you not
sign an injunction, that anyone who makes petition to any god or man within thirty days except
to you, O king, shall be cast into the den of lions?"
The king answered and said, "The thing stands fast,
according to the law of the Medes and Persians,
which cannot be revoked." Then they answered
and said before the king, "Daniel, who is one of
the exiles from Judah, pays no attention to you, O
king, or the injunction you have signed, but makes
his petition three times a day."

Then the king, when he heard these words, was
much distressed and set his mind to deliver Daniel.
And he labored till the sun went down to rescue him.
Then these men came by agreement to the king and
said to the king, "Know, O king, that it is a law of the
Medes and Persians that no injunction or ordinance
that the king establishes can be changed."

So far we have seen that Daniel, who is now somewhere around eighty years old, is once again part of a regime change. So he's dealing with a new king and a new empire.

But now we are going to see deep inside Daniel's life as he faces this crisis. In the process, we will discover the wellspring of his True Courage. Down deep, embedded in his heart, mind, and soul are old habits and ancient paths.

Now what do I mean by old habits and ancient paths? The text makes it very clear that when Daniel knew the document had been signed, he just went about life as he had always done. He obviously was well aware of the bill under consideration. Perhaps one of his friends on Gubaru's staff leaked it to him. But no matter—when he knew it had been signed into law, he just kept doing what he did every day. When he knew it was against the law to pray to the one true God, he just kept going on as though it wasn't against the law. He prayed three times a day when it was legal, and he wasn't going to stop now that it was illegal. When the laws of men violate the laws of God, you just keep obeying the law of God.

Even if it means paying the consequences.

Daniel was a man of habitual prayer. He was a man who had built spiritual disciplines into his life from his earliest days. Daily prayer had been a habit in his life for decades, and he wasn't about to stop now—even though he knew he'd been set up.

In fact, that was the secret of his True Courage.

In Philippians 4:9, Paul told the believers: "What you have learned and received and heard and seen in me—practice these things, and the God of peace will be with you." Not only is that true of Paul, it's true of Daniel as well. What we have learned and received and heard and seen in his life—we need to practice these things. They're not out of our reach. By God's help, they are within our reach.

Listen to the wise words of Martyn Lloyd-Jones:

> I have often observed when I read the biographies of saintly, godly men and women, that they always conform to a pattern. The saints are remarkably alike. If you read the life of any one of them, you will always find that their life was based on certain very simple principles. The saintly life is always a very simple life.... Here, then, are some of the principles by which the saints lived.... The first characteristic always of the saints was that they desired to live to (God's) glory.... Take any of the saints—Paul, Augustine, Luther, Calvin, Wesley—look at them, and you will see that this is the dominating feature of their lives. Yes, but let us be quite practical, how can we test whether this is true of us? "These things, which you have seen in me, do." What are they? First and foremost is reading the text book. If you would know God, then go to God's revelation....
>
> Then, next, obviously is prayer. If you like a person you want to spend as much time as you can with that person. If we want to know God better, surely we need to spend time talking to him.... You just start reading your Bible, and then you go and begin to pray. You may say, "But I can't pray." Then

talk to God about it. Tell him it is your desire to
know him better and to spend time with him.[3]

When you look closely at great men and women of God down
through the ages, the structure of their lives looks very similar. They
all had a certain consistency in their lives—that means they were all
on the path that leads to life. They were all walking on the road that
leads to the narrow gate. Or to put it another way, they were walking
the ancient paths.

Jeremiah 6:16 lays it out for us:

Thus says the LORD:

"Stand by the roads, and look,
     and ask for the ancient paths,

where the good way is; and walk in it,
     and find rest for your souls."

Certain men have chosen to walk with God. Enoch walked with
God. So did Abraham, Joseph, Moses, Elijah, Mordecai, and countless millions down through the ages. Even today, I know those who
walk with God. There are modern men and women with laptops
and iPhones, but they are individuals who have developed old habits
because they walk with God along the ancient paths.

Daniel had developed the habit of praying. In his case, he built
it into his schedule three times a day. Is that the way you must do it?
No, you can do it in the way that works best for you. But Lloyd-Jones

is right: *Just start talking to the Lord.* Tell Him what's on your heart; pour it all out to Him. Prayer really isn't for His benefit, it's for yours. Prayer is acknowledging that you are completely dependent upon Him. You can pray when you drive, or you can take a walk and talk to the Lord. Or you can write your prayer. Or you can take the prayers that Paul prayed in his letters and pray them, and insert your own name or someone else's name in those prayers. But whatever you do or however you do it, come to Him in Jesus' name and talk to Him. If you've sinned, however, confess it to Him and count on 1 John 1:9.

Keep coming to Him and talking with Him!

And keep your Bible open, and read it regularly.

These were old habits to Daniel, now that he was somewhere around eighty. My dad went home to be with the Lord last year. I have mentioned this in other books, and I mentioned it earlier in this one, but Dad was a man who had developed certain habits, and he practiced them for years. He would wake up early in the morning, get his coffee, grab his Bible, and spend the first hour or so of the day reading the Scripture, looking at a commentary or two, and praying. That's what he did every day. Not just some days, but *every* day. He died at eighty-five, but he started those habits way back some fifty or sixty years before.

And that's where I learned it. The habits that I learned and received and the truth that I heard and saw in him—those are the things that I am practicing in my own life. I'm grateful for my dad's example, and I'm grateful for the scriptural examples of Paul and Daniel. When you look at godly men in the past or the present, you always see the old habits as they walk the ancient path.

The Lion of lions rules over all other lions (Dan. 6:16–28).

Then the king commanded, and Daniel was brought and cast into the den of lions. The king declared to Daniel, "May your God, whom you serve continually, deliver you!" And a stone was brought and laid on the mouth of the den, and the king sealed it with his own signet and with the signet of his lords, that nothing might be changed concerning Daniel. Then the king went to his palace and spent the night fasting; no diversions were brought to him, and sleep fled from him.

Then, at break of day, the king arose and went in haste to the den of lions. As he came near to the den where Daniel was, he cried out in a tone of anguish. The king declared to Daniel, "O Daniel, servant of the living God, has your God, whom you serve continually, been able to deliver you from the lions?" Then Daniel said to the king, "O king, live forever! My God sent his angel and shut the lions' mouths, and they have not harmed me, because I was found blameless before him; and also before you, O king, I have done no harm." Then the king was exceedingly glad, and commanded that Daniel be taken up out of the den. So Daniel was taken up out of the den, and no kind of harm was found on him, because he had trusted in his God. And the king commanded, and those men who had

maliciously accused Daniel were brought and cast
into the den of lions—they, their children, and
their wives. And before they reached the bottom of
the den, the lions overpowered them and broke all
their bones in pieces. (vv. 16–24)

This is one of the most famous stories in all of the Bible. But I
want to note a couple of things about Daniel's amazing deliverance.

1. Daniel was delivered, but his accusers and their families were not.
That just doesn't seem right, and it wasn't right. So what's the
explanation? John C. Whitcomb summed it up best:

The God of Israel gave a law to His people through
Moses that children "should not be put to death for
their fathers; everyone shall be put to death for his
own sin" (Deuteronomy 24:16; cf. 2 Kings 14:6). If
Achan's entire family was stoned to death for his sin,
it was because all of them were active participants
with the head of the household in this particular sin
(Joshua 7:24–26).

But the Medo-Persians had no such merciful
law. Wives, children, and other relatives were often
killed at the king's command when a man committed a serious crime against the royal house, thus
"nipping in the bud" any possible retaliation by the
criminal's family (to say nothing of the deterrent
that such drastic justice would provide for potential
enemies).[4]

2. Another pagan is brought to a place of giving glory to Daniel's sovereign and all-powerful God.

It's clear from the text that something had happened in the life of Darius before he put Daniel in the lions' den. Back in verse 16, as Daniel was about to be thrown into that den of death, Darius acknowledged that the God whom Daniel constantly served had the power to deliver His servant. What was it that had brought this about? No doubt he had heard firsthand about the handwriting on the wall that brought down Belshazzar. And we can be pretty sure he knew all about the God who came down to walk with His faithful followers in the fiery furnace.

But did he truly fear and revere the Lord, the God of Israel? This testimony puts it all to rest.

> Then King Darius wrote to all the peoples, nations, and languages that dwell in all the earth: "Peace be multiplied to you. I make a decree, that in all my royal dominion people are to tremble and fear before the God of Daniel,
>
> for he is the living God,
> > enduring forever;
>
> his kingdom shall never be destroyed,
> > and his dominion shall be to the end.
>
> He delivers and rescues;
> > he works signs and wonders
> > in heaven and on earth,

he who has saved Daniel

from the power of the lions." (Dan. 6:25–27)

MY VISIT TO THE LIONS' DEN

Over the last three years, I have found myself in the lions' den. Details aren't necessary, except to say that I was facing a situation that could have been devastating. It looked liked it would be resolved, and then it would rear up again. On and on this continued. At first, it looked like it would be handled within a few months—and then it was delayed. It would start again and then be delayed again. The pressure was potentially suffocating and the consequences potentially cataclysmic. My goal in this was to not let worry and fear dominate me. So whenever the fear would show up, I would absolutely refuse to give in and worry about it. I would immediately remind myself of scriptures that spoke of God's power and sovereignty.

Those scriptures were my sword (Eph. 6:17), and along with my other pieces of armor, they enabled me to sleep well at night.

One particular night I experienced a stronger wave of attack than ever before. So I strapped on my armor and got out my sword, and before long my mind and heart were quieted in the goodness and power of God, and I went to sleep.

And then I woke up.

And my first conscious thought was Isaiah 30.

I don't mean it was my third thought or my seventh. The moment I came out of that sleep, Isaiah 30 was waiting for me.

I'll be honest with you: Scripture isn't usually my first thought in the morning. My first thought is normally *Where am I?* or *Am I breathing?* or *Which way to the bathroom?* That's my normal first moments of consciousness. But not on this morning. Isaiah 30 was on my mind, and the Spirit of God had obviously put it there. I didn't hear a voice, and I didn't have a vision. It was just Isaiah 30.

Back in the '60s, there was a band called We Five who had one hit. The first line of the song was, "When I woke up this morning, you were on my mind." The group didn't last long, but if they were still around, I would tell them that I woke up that morning, and Isaiah 30 was on my mind.

I got out of bed, went into my study, grabbed my Bible, dropped into the nearest chair, and opened to Isaiah 30. I read the whole chapter. The context was that the nation of Judah greatly feared the Assyrian king and his bloodthirsty army. So they cashed in their IRAs and 401(k)s and went down to Egypt to try and buy the protection of the Egyptian king and his army. Instead of trusting in God to deliver them from the Assyrian lions, they went running down to Egypt. But why? Why go to Egypt when you have a great and sovereign God who has promised to protect the nation? So that was the context—and I was drawn to the words of verse 15, where God tells them to repent and return to Him:

For thus said the Lord GOD, the Holy One of Israel,

"In returning and rest you shall be saved;
    in quietness and in trust shall be your strength."

As I was mulling that over in my mind, I thought to myself, *I wonder what Leupold has to say about this verse?* I have a bunch of commentaries in my study, including quite a few on Isaiah, but for some reason H. C. Leupold's commentary on Isaiah came to my mind. I reached over, grabbed the volume, and started reading. When I got to verse 15, I read Leupold's translation and then his comments:

> For thus says the LORD, the Holy One of Israel;
> "If you return and wait calmly, you will be rescued;
>   if you remain quiet and maintain confidence, you
>   will be strong."

God was telling Israel that they should not seek out the king of Egypt to save them from the massive armies of the king of Assyria. Leupold said that their hope was in alliances rather than on the living God, and they couldn't be more wrong. They needed to depend upon the Lord instead of alliances with other nations. In speaking of their returning to the Lord, instead of counting on their alliance with Egypt, Leupold wrote:

> After this alliance is abandoned, then it behooves the nation to "wait calmly." *There are times when the danger threatening is beyond man's ability to control the situation. All that is left to do is to wait on the Lord.* Such a situation prevails in this case. This is further spelled out as involving "to remain quiet and maintain confidence." If this approach is used,

the nation will ultimately be "rescued" and at the same time it will "be strong." *For seemingly passive reliance on the Lord is not weakness, it is actually strength.* [italics mine][5]

What struck me about this paragraph is the fact that we are thrown into situations where the danger threatening is beyond man's ability to control the situation. In other words, there is no hope unless God comes through. That's exactly what happened to Daniel as he was thrown to the lions.

And I almost forgot—did you notice the last sentence of that quote from Leupold? *"For seemingly passive reliance on the Lord is not weakness, it is actually strength."* I need to point something out about his statement. Did you catch it?

It's counterintuitive.

What seems to be passive reliance is not being weak—it is in reality great strength—it's a demonstration of True Courage. There it is: We started this book with it, and we are ending with it. True Courage is counterintuitive.

There are three sane yet counterintuitive steps to take when life is out of our control and you are threatened by the lions.

- Wait calmly
- Remain quiet
- Maintain confidence

That sums up the message of Isaiah 30:15. And it fits perfectly with what we have seen in Daniel's life. I have found that those three nuggets provide great ballast to the unrelenting emotional upheaval of fear and anxiety.

God will make a way—and while I'm looking to Him for His answer, I must *wait calmly, remain quiet,* and *maintain confidence.*

So what does that look like practically speaking?

When Daniel was shown the shocking events that would take place in the last days, he was sick and exhausted (Dan. 8:27). And then what did he do? He got up and went to work.

It was a tragic time when all of the families of Judah were taken from their homes to join Daniel in Babylon. They knew that they would be in a foreign land for seventy years. And to those worried people God gave some very clear direction in Jeremiah 29:4–7. It was remarkably practical and down to earth. He told them to build houses and plant organic gardens. He told the men to take wives and to have kids. And then they were to help their kids find godly mates so that they could marry and have kids.

It doesn't get any more practical than that.

In other words, they were to trust God and keep living life.

He would be the stability of their times, and He will be the stability of our times (Isa. 33:6 NASB).

It is our responsibility to believe that and to live in those truths each day.

And that is the essence of True Courage.

NOTES

INTRODUCTION: TROUBLED HEARTS AND TRUE COURAGE

1. Arthur C. Brooks, *The Battle* (New York: Basic, 2010), 3.

2. J. I. Packer, Merrill C. Tenney, William White Jr., *The Bible Almanac* (Nashville, TN: Thomas Nelson, 1980), 263.

3. Wayne Grudem, *Politics—According to the Bible* (Grand Rapids, MI: Zondervan, 2010), 261–62.

4. *The ESV Study Bible*, "Introduction to Jeremiah" (Wheaton, IL: Crossway, 2008), 1364.

CHAPTER 1: COURAGE TO STAY THE COURSE

1. C. F. Keil and F. Delitzsch, *Commentary on the Old Testament in Ten Volumes*, vol. 9 (Grand Rapids, MI: William B. Eerdmans, 1980), 79.

2. Daymond R. Duck and Larry Richards, *The Book of Daniel* (Nashville, TN: Thomas Nelson, 2007), 13.

3. D. Martyn Lloyd-Jones, *Healing and the Scriptures* (Nashville, TN: Oliver Nelson, 1982), 103.

4. C. J. Mahaney, *Humility* (Sisters, OR: Multnomah, 2005), 22.

CHAPTER 2: ACTS AND FACTS

1. Harry Blamires, *The Christian Mind* (Ann Arbor, MI: Servant, 1978), 110–11.

2. Ibid., 67.

3. Paul Johnston, *Churchill* (New York: Viking, 2009), 3.

4. Chartwell Booksellers, www.churchillbooks.com/contact.cfm (accessed November 23, 2010).

5. Winston Churchill, as quoted in "Great Prime Ministers," *LIFE,* May 24, 1948, 74.

6. Winston Churchill, as quoted in Richard Langworth, *Churchill by Himself* (New York: Public Affairs, 2008), 465.

7. Celia Lee and John Lee, *The Churchills: A Family Portrait* (New York: Palgrave Macmillan, 2010), 49.

8. Churchill, as quoted in Langworth, *Churchill by Himself,* 595.

9. Billy Graham, *Just As I Am* (New York: HarperCollins, 1997), 235–37.

10. See "M'Cheyne's One-Year Reading Plan" at www.esv.org/biblereadingplans (accessed November 23, 2010).

CHAPTER 3: FLUMMOXED AND FLABBERGASTED

1. Paul Johnson, *Heroes* (New York: HarperCollins, 2007), 40.

2. *The ESV Study Bible* (Wheaton, IL: Crossway, 2008), 1588.

3. John Newton, as quoted in Iain H. Murray, *Heroes* (Carlisle, PA: The Banner of Truth Trust, 2009), 99.

4. Mitch Stokes, *Isaac Newton* (Nashville, TN: Thomas Nelson, 2010), 42–43.

5. Ibid., 44.

6. Ibid., 54.

7. Bruce K. Waltke, *An Old Testament Theology* (Grand Rapids, MI: Zondervan, 2007), 9.

8. Ibid., 12.

CHAPTER 4: GOLD STANDARD

1. Dan Simon, "The gambling man who co-founded Apple and left for $800," CNN, www.cnn.com/2010/TECH/web/06/24/apple. forgotten.founder/index.html?hpt=C2 (accessed November 24, 2010).

2. David S. Kidder and Noah D. Oppenheim, *The Intellectual Devotional: Biographies* (New York: Rodale, 2010), 296, as cited in Anthony Gottlieb, "A Nervous Splendor," *The New Yorker,* www.newyorker.com/ arts/critics/books/2009/04/06/090406crbo_books_gottlieb (accessed November 24, 2010).

3. Benjamin Breckenridge Warfield, *The Works of Benjamin B. Warfield,* vol. 2 (Grand Rapids, MI: Baker, 1981), 8–9.

4. Ibid., 9.

5. John Newton, as quoted in Iain H. Murray, *Heroes* (Carlisle, PA: The Banner of Truth Trust, 2009), 96.

6. Warren Wiersbe, *The Bible Exposition Commentary: Prophets* (Colorado Springs: Victor, 2002), 260.

7. *The ESV Study Bible* (Wheaton, IL: Crossway, 2008), 1590.

8. John F. Walvoord and Roy B. Zuck, *The Bible Knowledge Commentary: Old Testament* (Wheaton, IL: Victor, 1983), 1099.

9. John S. Feinberg, *No One Like Him* (Wheaton, IL: Crossway, 2001), xxv, italics mine.

10. Wiersbe, *The Bible Exposition Commentary: Prophets,* 261.

11. J. Vernon McGee, *Thru the Bible with J. Vernon McGee,* vol. 3 (Nashville, TN: Thomas Nelson, 1982), 541.

12. John MacArthur, "The Theology of Sleep! (Mark 4)," Vimeo, http://vimeo.com/10941231 (accessed November 24, 2010).

CHAPTER 5: LOCK, STOCK, AND BARREL

1. John H. Lienhard, "Engines of Our Ingenuity: Interchangeable Parts," University of Houston, www.uh.edu/engines/epi1252.htm (accessed November 29, 2010).

2. Patricia Ryaby Backer, "Industrialization of American Society," Engineering at San Jose University, www.engr.sjsu.edu/pabacker/industrial.htm (accessed November 29, 2010), par. 8.

3. Thomas Jefferson and John P. Foley, *The Jeffersonian Cyclopedia* (London–New York: Funk & Wagnalls, 1900), 600.

4. Kenneth Hopper and William Hopper, *The Puritan Gift* (London–New York: I. B. Tauris, 2009), 43.

5. P. B. Power, *The "I Wills" of the Psalms* (Carlisle, PA: The Banner of Truth Trust, 1848; 1985), 2.

6. Charles Dyer and Gene Merrill, *The Old Testament Explorer* (Nashville, TN: Word, 2001), 613.

7. Martin Heidegger, as quoted in Peter Hitchens, *The Rage Against God* (Grand Rapids, MI: Zondervan, 2010), 148.

8. *The ESV Study Bible* (Wheaton, IL: Crossway, 2007), 69.

9. Charles Dyer and Angela Elwell Hunt, *The Rise of Babylon* (Wheaton, IL: Tyndale, 1991), 17–18.

10. Daniel Yergin and Joseph Stanislaw, *The Commanding Heights* (New York: Simon & Schuster, 1998), 69.

11. Joyce G. Baldwin, *Daniel: An Introduction and Commentary* (Downers Grove, IL: InterVarsity, 1978), 99.

12. John Calvin, Calvin's Commentaries, vol. 12, *Daniel* (Grand Rapids, MI: Baker, 1979), 1:220.

13. Cyprian, as quoted in John Calvin, Calvin's Commentaries, vol. 12, *Daniel,* 1:220.

14. Robert Duncan Culver, *Systematic Theology: Biblical and Historical* (Ross-shire, UK: Mentor, 2005), 442–43.

15. George Müller, *Autobiography of George Müller* (Denton, TX: Westminster Literature Resources, 2003), 368.

CHAPTER 6: THE HARD WAY

1. Peter Hitchens, *The Rage Against God* (Grand Rapids, MI: Zondervan, 2010), 17–18.

2. Jonathan Aitken, *John Newton* (Wheaton, IL: Crossway, 2007), 58.

3. John Newton, as quoted in Iain H. Murray, *Heroes* (Carlisle, PA: The Banner of Truth Trust, 2009), 97.

4. Ibid., 92.

5. C. S. Lewis, *Mere Christianity* (San Francisco: HarperSanFrancisco, 1952), 121–22, 124.

6. G. K. Chesterton, *Orthodoxy* (Nashville, TN: Sam Torode, 2009), 89.

7. Thomas Watson, *A Body of Divinity* (Carlisle, PA: The Banner of Truth Trust, 1692; 1958), 7.

8. David McCullough, *Brave Companions* (New York: Touchstone, 1992), 118.

9. Ibid., 123.

10. C. H. Spurgeon, "The Obedience of Faith," Metropolitan Tabernacle Pulpit, Spurgeon.org, www.spurgeon.org/sermons/2195.htm (accessed November 30, 2010), par. 5.

CHAPTER 7: A SLIGHT THING

1. John Flavel, *The Mystery of Providence* (Carlisle, PA: The Banner of Truth Trust, 1678; 1963), 34.

2. Ibid., 34, 40.

3. R. C. Sproul and Keith Mathison, eds., *The Reformation Study Bible* (Orlando, FL: Ligonier, 2005), 518.

4. Daymond R. Duck and Larry Richards, *The Book of Daniel* (Nashville, TN: Thomas Nelson, 2007), 125–26.

5. Ibid., 126.

6. Ibid., 144–45.

7. Gleason L. Archer, *A Survey of Old Testament Introduction* (Chicago: Moody, 1994), 429.

8. Ibid., 385.

9. Stanley Marcus, *The Viewpoints of Stanley Marcus* (Denton, TX: University of North Texas, 1995), 57–58, as quoted in Kenneth Hopper and William Hopper, *The Puritan Gift* (London–New York: I. B. Tauris, 2009), 167.

10. Hopper and Hopper, *The Puritan Gift,* 169.

11. David Jeremiah, *The Prophecy Answer Book* (Nashville, TN: Thomas Nelson, 2010), 14–15.

CHAPTER 8: IN THE COMPANY OF LIONS

1. I am indebted to Keith Mathison for making me aware of Morgan Robertson and *The Wreck of the Titan.* In his excellent article entitled "Mere Coincidence," he also referenced the quote on Providence from the Westminster Confession of Faith. His article can be found at: www.ligonier.org/learn/articles/mere-coincidence (accessed December 1, 2010).

2. Gleason L. Archer, *Encyclopedia of Bible Difficulties* (Grand Rapids, MI: Zondervan, 1982), 288.

3. D. Martyn Lloyd-Jones, *The Life of Peace* (Grand Rapids, MI: Baker, 1990), 197–99.

4. John C. Whitcomb, *Everyman's Bible Commentary: Daniel* (Chicago: Moody, 1985), 88.

5. H. C. Leupold, *Exposition of Isaiah* (Grand Rapids, MI: Baker, 1976), 475.